Home Network Security Simplified

P9-DOB-026

Jim Doherty

Neil Anderson

Illustrations by Nathan Clement

Cisco Press
800 East 96th Street
Indianapolis, IN 46240

LONGWOOD PUBLIC LIBRARY

Home Network Security Simplified

Jim Doherty

Neil Anderson

Copyright© 2007 Cisco Systems, Inc.

Published by:
Cisco Press
800 East 96th Street
Indianapolis, IN 46240 USA

All rights reserved. No part of this book may be reproduced or transmitted in any form or by any means, electronic or mechanical, including photocopying, recording, or by any information storage and retrieval system, without written permission from the publisher, except for the inclusion of brief quotations in a review.

Printed in the United States of America 1 2 3 4 5 6 7 8 9 0

First Printing   July 2006

ISBN: 1-58720-163-1

Library of Congress Cataloging-in-Publication Data

Doherty, Jim, CCNA.
  Home network security simplified / Jim Doherty and Neil Anderson.
     p. cm.
  Includes index.
  ISBN 1-58720-163-1 (pbk.)
  1. Home computer networks--Security measures. I. Anderson, Neil, 1965- II. Title.
  TK5105.75.D638 2007
  005.8--dc22

                          2006019633

Warning and Disclaimer

This book is designed to provide information about home network security. Every effort has been made to make this book as complete and as accurate as possible, but no warranty or fitness is implied.

The information is provided on an "as is" basis. The authors, Cisco Press, and Cisco Systems, Inc. shall have neither liability nor responsibility to any person or entity with respect to any loss or damages arising from the information contained in this book or from the use of the discs or programs that may accompany it.

The opinions expressed in this book belong to the author and are not necessarily those of Cisco Systems, Inc.

Feedback Information

At Cisco Press, our goal is to create in-depth technical books of the highest quality and value. Each book is crafted with care and precision, undergoing rigorous development that involves the unique expertise of members from the professional technical community.

Readers' feedback is a natural continuation of this process. If you have any comments regarding how we could improve the quality of this book, or otherwise alter it to better suit your needs, you can contact us through email at feedback@ciscopress.com. Please make sure to include the book title and ISBN in your message.

We greatly appreciate your assistance.

Trademark Acknowledgments

All terms mentioned in this book that are known to be trademarks or service marks have been appropriately capitalized. Cisco Press or Cisco Systems, Inc. cannot attest to the accuracy of this information. Use of a term in this book should not be regarded as affecting the validity of any trademark or service mark.

CISCO SYSTEMS

Corporate Headquarters
Cisco Systems, Inc.
170 West Tasman Drive
San Jose, CA 95134-1706
USA
www.cisco.com
Tel: 408 526-4000
　　800 553-NETS (6387)
Fax: 408 526-4100

European Headquarters
Cisco Systems International BV
Haarlerbergpark
Haarlerbergweg 13-19
1101 CH Amsterdam
The Netherlands
www-europe.cisco.com
Tel: 31 0 20 357 1000
Fax: 31 0 20 357 1100

Americas Headquarters
Cisco Systems, Inc.
170 West Tasman Drive
San Jose, CA 95134-1706
USA
www.cisco.com
Tel: 408 526-7660
Fax: 408 527-0883

Asia Pacific Headquarters
Cisco Systems, Inc.
Capital Tower
168 Robinson Road
#22-01 to #29-01
Singapore 068912
www.cisco.com
Tel: +65 6317 7777
Fax: +65 6317 7799

Cisco Systems has more than 200 offices in the following countries and regions. Addresses, phone numbers, and fax numbers are listed on the
Cisco.com Web site at www.cisco.com/go/offices.

Argentina • Australia • Austria • Belgium • Brazil • Bulgaria • Canada • Chile • China PRC • Colombia • Costa Rica • Croatia • Czech Republic
Denmark • Dubai, UAE • Finland • France • Germany • Greece • Hong Kong SAR • Hungary • India • Indonesia • Ireland • Israel • Italy
Japan • Korea • Luxembourg • Malaysia • Mexico • The Netherlands • New Zealand • Norway • Peru • Philippines • Poland • Portugal
Puerto Rico • Romania • Russia • Saudi Arabia • Scotland • Singapore • Slovakia • Slovenia • South Africa • Spain • Sweden
Switzerland • Taiwan • Thailand • Turkey • Ukraine • United Kingdom • United States • Venezuela • Vietnam • Zimbabwe

Copyright © 2003 Cisco Systems, Inc. All rights reserved. CCIP, CCSP, the Cisco Arrow logo, the Cisco *Powered* Network mark, the Cisco Systems Verified logo, Cisco Unity, Follow Me Browsing, FormShare, iQ Net Readiness Scorecard, Networking Academy, and ScriptShare are trademarks of Cisco Systems, Inc.; Changing the Way We Work, Live, Play, and Learn, The Fastest Way to Increase Your Internet Quotient, and iQuick Study are service marks of Cisco Systems, Inc.; and Aironet, ASIST, BPX, Catalyst, CCDA, CCDP, CCIE, CCNA, CCNP, Cisco, the Cisco Certified Internetwork Expert logo, Cisco IOS, the Cisco IOS logo, Cisco Press, Cisco Systems, Cisco Systems Capital, the Cisco Systems logo, Empowering the Internet Generation, Enterprise/Solver, EtherChannel, EtherSwitch, Fast Step, GigaStack, Internet Quotient, IOS, IP/TV, iQ Expertise, the iQ logo, LightStream, MGX, MICA, the Networkers logo, Network Registrar, *Packet*, PIX, Post-Routing, Pre-Routing, RateMUX, Registrar, SlideCast, SMARTnet, StrataView Plus, Stratm, SwitchProbe, TeleRouter, TransPath, and VCO are registered trademarks of Cisco Systems, Inc. and/or its affiliates in the U.S. and certain other countries.

All other trademarks mentioned in this document or Web site are the property of their respective owners. The use of the word partner does not imply a partnership relationship between Cisco and any other company. (0303R)

Printed in the USA

Publisher
Paul Boger

Cisco Representative
Anthony Wolfenden

**Cisco Press
Program Manager**
Jeff Brady

Senior Editor
Elizabeth Peterson

Managing Editor
Patrick Kanouse

Development Editor
Andrew Cupp

Senior Project Editor
San Dee Phillips

Project Editor
Betsy Harris

Copy Editor
Keith Cline

Technical Editors
Doug Foster
Bradley Mitchell

Editorial Assistant
Vanessa Evans

Cover Designer
Louisa Adair

**Book Designer
and Compositor**
Mark Shirar

Indexer
Tim Wright

Proofreader
Katherin Bidwell

About the Authors

Jim Doherty is the director of marketing and programs with Symbol Technologies' industry solutions group. Prior to joining Symbol, Jim worked at Cisco Systems, where he led various marketing campaigns for IP telephony and routing and switching solutions. Jim has 17 years of engineering and marketing experience across a broad range of networking and communications technologies. Jim is the co-author of the *Networking Simplified* series of books, including *Cisco Networking Simplified*, *Home Networking Simplified*, and *Internet Phone Services Simplified*. He is also the author of the "Study Notes" section of *CCNA Flash Cards and Exam Practice Pack* (CCNA Self-Study, Exam #640-801), Second Edition. Jim is a former Marine Corps sergeant; he holds a bachelor of science degree in electrical engineering from North Carolina State University and an MBA from Duke University.

Neil Anderson is the senior manager of enterprise systems engineering with Cisco Systems. Neil has more than 20 years of broad engineering experience, including public telephone systems, mobile phone systems, Internet, and home networking. At Cisco, Neil's focus is on large corporate customers in the areas of routing and switching, wireless, security, and IP communications. Neil is the co-author of the *Networking Simplified* series of books including, *Home Networking Simplified* and *Internet Phone Services Simplified*. Neil holds a bachelor of science degree in computer science.

About the Illustrator

Nathan Clement declared himself an illustrator a little more than three years ago. Nathan holds a bachelor of fine arts degree in art and writing, which launched a surprise career in publishing, design, and art direction. His major roles have been owning a printing company, designing books in-house at Macmillan Computer Publishing, and serving as art director for an ad agency. Through these little adventures, he decided to get back to his art roots and keep both feet planted in the publishing world as an illustrator. He has been pleased to illustrate three previous books in the Cisco Press *Networking Simplified* series and has done work for Que Publishing, Macromedia Press, Peachpit Press, Prentice Hall, and *ESPN The Magazine*. He lives with his wife, Greta, a nurse practitioner, in Indianapolis and also pursues children's book illustration with paint and brushes. Contact Nathan at nathan@stickman-studio.com.

About the Technical Reviewers

Doug Foster works in the area of packet voice, video, and data convergence. With 30 years of experience for companies such as Cisco Systems, John Deere, Alcatel, and private business, Doug has some interesting firsthand stories to tell about the evolution of the Internet. He has architected and helped install international networks—such as the migration of John Deere's worldwide SNA business network into a multiprotocol intranet in the mid-1980s. As a result of that work, Doug was asked by the U.S. Department of Defense to speak at Interop '88 on "How John Deere builds tractors using TCP/IP." This was nearly a decade before most businesses began to leverage the value of the Internet and eCommerce applications. Most recently, Doug worked for Cisco Systems as one of its first enterprise voice consultants.

Doug has a bachelor of science in mechanical engineering from Iowa State University and lives in Cary, North Carolina, with his wife, Cindy. When not busy with family—daughters, Erin and Amber; son-in-law, Jeremy; and grandson, Jake—or business (Convinsys, Performance Podcasts, and Idea Mechanics), Doug devotes his free time to writing his first book (*Convince Me!*) and to sea kayaking.

Bradley Mitchell works as a freelance writer on the About.com wireless/networking site. He has produced online content at About.com on home computer networking, wireless, and related topics for six years. Bradley is also a senior engineer at Intel Corporation. Over the past 12 years at Intel, he has served in various capacities for research and development of software and network systems. Bradley obtained his master's degree in computer science from the University of Illinois and his bachelor's degree from M.I.T.

Dedications

I would like to dedicate this book to my parents, Jim Doherty and Pierrette Phillips. Dad, thanks for teaching me to be a good kid. Mom, thanks for sticking up for me when I wasn't.

—Jim

I would like to dedicate this book to my parents. I am not exactly sure how, but my dad continues to live in the twenty-first century without touching a computer. That's one way to avoid online identity theft. And to my mom, who despite being the target of several computer viruses, still sees the value in home and business networking.

—Neil

Acknowledgments

Jim and Neil would like to thank the following people:

Our families, for putting up with all the late nights and weekends, rooms full of computers and cables, and for changes we made to their PCs when they were asleep or at school.

Our publisher and the fine team at Cisco Press and Pearson Education. We would especially like to thank our editor, Drew Cupp, who we beat like a rented mule. He not only survived, he also managed to make sense out of our garbled English.

Our illustrator, Nathan Clement at Stickman Studios (www.stickman-studio.com/), who makes all this stuff come to life with great illustrations.

Our technical reviewers, Bradley Mitchell and Doug Foster, who both make sure we do our homework and who keep us from making fools of ourselves by catching our mistakes before you ever see them.

And last but not least, the following people who helped us with technical questions along the way: Stuart Hamilton, Steve Ochmanski, Brian Cox, Lou Ronnau, Max Ardica, and Jason Frazier.

Contents at a Glance

Contents

Introduction

This book provides what we hope is a simplified approach to home network security. Our aim is not to make you a security expert or a network expert or an expert on any other topic. We would, however, like to arm you with some amount of knowledge and know-how so that you can adequately protect your assets (monetary and computer) and identity, which are both at risk when you connect your computer to the Internet. Some level of risk is always present while on the Internet, but the danger can be mitigated. Without knowing what the threats are and how to protect yourself against them, you put yourself in an unnecessarily risky position. Most books on security try to hook you with fear: fear of hackers, fear of viruses, fear of some digital terrorist stealing your credit card numbers and buying an island in the Caribbean. Our approach is different. The best tool for fighting fear is knowledge; knowledge of the real threats (not the hype), knowledge of the types of security available, and probably most important, knowledge of what to do to keep yourself reasonably safe from threats.

We provide this knowledge in the form of actionable steps that you can take to protect yourself. Ten things that, if done correctly, will keep you safe against the most common threats, attacks, hacks, and scams. Will following these 10 steps make your home network 100 percent bulletproof? Not a chance. The only true way to be 100 percent bulletproof is to turn off your computer and bury it in the backyard. But if you do follow these 10 steps, it will give you a reasonable level of security, keeping you about as safe as one can be without becoming a full-fledged security expert and spending a bunch of money.

Why Do I Even Need Network Security in the First Place?

We promised not to jump on the fear-mongering bandwagon, but we do need to help you 1) recognize that threats do exist and 2) understand the nature of the threats so that you can adequately protect yourselves against them. First things first: the threats.

Unless you have been living in a cave for some time (and even then, maybe), you have surely heard about the threat of computer viruses, worms, hackers, scams, and identity thefts. Internet security is big news, and also big business. On a corporate level, companies must protect themselves against intrusion attempts aimed at gaining secret information, and against attempts to shut down corporate websites that provide both the face of a company and a revenue conduit. On the home network side, individuals must protect their personal information, protect their computers from corruption or from being taken over, and protect against others accessing their networks to download illegal or illicit material (or just annoying the heck out of you with endless spam).

If you do connect to the Internet, sooner or later you will see every threat and hack attempt there is. Well, you'll see it if you take no precautions. If you follow the steps we lay out, you will either stop them in the act by recognizing the threat and acting accordingly or prevent them from happening at all and not even be bothered by it.

Threat Categories

One of the things that we have noticed in most of the books and articles on home network security is a lack of any explanation of the different types of security threats. This is a pretty serious issue because many nonexperts lump every type of threat into something called "security," which often leads people into thinking that one type of security solution, say a firewall, will protect them from all the bad stuff out there. This is a big mistake. There are several different types of security threats and one or two things that you can and should do for each type of threat. To help you sort it out, we have grouped threats into four basic categories: connection-based threats, access-based threats, software-based threats, and victim-enabled threats. Each threat category is described here.

Connection-Based Threats

A connection-based threat is an attack that is directed through your Internet connection. This threat exists because high-speed Internet is always on (unlike dialup, which you set up, use, and then break the connection when finished). Hackers typically look for open IP addresses (which represent your location on the Internet) using tools that randomly look for an open connection into an unprotected home network. When hackers find an open network, they can do a number of bad things, including but not limited to, searching through and possibly deleting personal information and files; or using your computer to launch attacks against other home, commercial, or government networks. This latter form of activity is called a redirect attack, a tactic hackers use to protect their own identity and location.

Access-Based Threats

An access-based threat usually results from using a wireless networking device in your home. Just about every wireless router on the market today is made to work right out of the box. This is great for getting your wireless networking up and running quickly, but the only way to make it that easy for you is to turn off all the security features, which makes is easy for everyone else in range of the router to gain access to your network, too. The usual result of not guarding against this threat is that you end up providing all the people around you with free Internet access. This may or may not be an issue for you, but you are also vulnerable to some hackers who can access your files or monitor your network traffic looking for passwords and personal information such as credit card numbers. There is also the risk that someone might be looking to download illicit, indecent, or illegal (sometime all three simultaneously) material from the Internet through your network rather than their own, just in case the feds or someone else come looking for them.

Software-Based Threats

This is probably the threat most people are familiar with. The category includes viruses, worms, spam, spyware, adware, and Trojan horses. Most of the time, these types of attacks are more of an inconvenience than anything else, but the annoyance factor gets pretty high when you get 100 or so unsolicited e-mails every day or if a virus copies your entire contacts list and starts sending copies of itself to everyone you know. Some viruses, though, can damage your computer or files, or worse, deposit a Trojan horse that enables a hacker to take remote control of your computer. All should be guarded against.

Victim-Enabled Threats

The Internet is a scam artist's paradise. Along with the usual array of rip-off scams, the Internet allows thieves to wrap themselves in legitimate-looking letters, web pages, and other wrappers that make it hard for the casual observer to tell the difference between legitimate and illegitimate sites and sources. The good news is that it takes a victim's participation to enable these threats. Unlike the other threats that require hardware or software, this type of threat can usually be solved with a simple set of rules for answering account questions and some education on how to avoid biting on the bait. In addition to identity theft, there is also good old-fashioned theft (someone taking your laptop), so we also provide you with some tips on how to keep folks from cracking your passwords.

Some of the threats we discuss actually fall into more than one category, and we point those out to you as we go. In addition, we have put a little summary box at the beginning of each chapter that describes the threat, what the issues are, and what you can do about it.

What's to Come?

The rest of this book is set up such that each chapter provides a security tip that you should follow. In each chapter, we describe the category of threat protection and give an example or two of common threats. Nothing too deep, as you really do not need to know, for example, how a virus works in a detailed way; you just need to know how to recognize the threat and, most important, how to protect yourself against it. We also provide a detailed explanation about how to use the hardware, install the software, what to be suspicious of, and when to unplug everything and maybe just go outside and play with the kids.

We recommend that you follow all 10 tips because they all guard against different threats within the 4 threat categories.

To get you started, here is an illustration that describes each threat and shows you the relevant topics. After that, we get right to the business of keeping you, your stuff, and your bank account safe from the bad guys.

The Internet

Access-Based Threats
Topics Include:
• Wireless Security
• Antivirus

Wireless Router

Connection-Based Threats
Topics Include:
• Firewalls
• Spyware/Adware

You and Your Computer

Victim-Enabled Threats
Topics Include:
• Phishing Scams
• Common Sense
• Child Protection

Software-Based Threats
Topics Include:
• OS Upgrades
• File Backups
• Antivirus

Please send your:
✓ Password
✓ Bank Account Number
✓ Picture and Address

Housekeeping Stuff

This book focuses on the Windows operating systems, and all screen shots were taken from computers running Windows XP Home Edition. If you are not running Windows XP Home Edition, you can still follow the recommendations and tips for the chapters where changes or setups are made or where directory paths are followed. The general steps still hold, but the directory paths and filenames might vary. Your User Manual or help files should help get you where you need to go. In some places, we give special instructions for other operating systems, too.

We also had to make some decisions regarding what type of hardware or programs to install as examples. These are our obvious recommendations, but we also mention good alternatives regarding security equipment or programs. In most cases, turning on the security measures we point out with any equipment fitting the category will be a huge step up from doing nothing at all. When we do make a recommendation, it is usually based on price and performance reasons.

We are not being paid by any of the vendors we refer to in the book, and we do not endorse any particular products. When we do call out and show examples with a specific product, it's because we need to show a tangible example to illustrate how to protect against the security threat being discussed. Feel free to try out the products we show or research and try others.

CHAPTER 1

Tip 1: Use Firewalls

Threat Type: Connection based, software based

Examples of Threats:

- Unauthorized access to your home network or a computer on your home network through your Internet connection

- Unauthorized installation of software programs onto a computer or device on your home network

- Unauthorized access by a computer or software program to the Internet, exchanging unintended information

- Using compromised computers on your home network as anonymous sources for launching attacks on others

Our Tips:

- Install a stateful-packet-inspection firewall between your broadband Internet connection and home network.

- Install personal firewall software on each of the computers in your home network.

- Periodically monitor access logs and firewall rules to ensure continued protection.

The term *firewall* is borrowed from the construction industry, where a hardened fire-proof material, such as cinder block, is built between two sections of a building so that if one catches on fire, the other might not.

A firewall in computer terms provides similar protection, by shielding one part of a network (say, your home network) from another part (say, the Internet) that may be "on fire." Now, the Internet is not exactly in flames, but it is a "dirty" network, meaning few rules and regulations apply, and those that do exist are often circumvented by some folks. You can view the Internet kind of like the Wild West of networks.

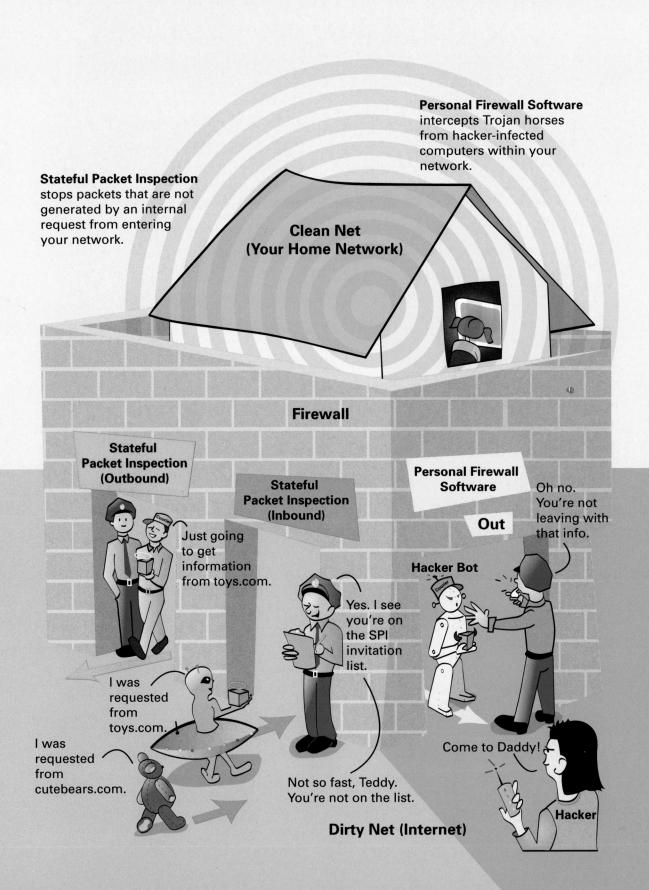

Firewalls are one of the most important lines of defense you need for your home network. You may ask yourself, "Why are firewalls so important? After all, I have been using the Internet for years with a dialup connection and never needed one before."

The answer is simple. If you only have to go into a bad part of town occasionally, maybe you can just be careful. If you have to live in that part of town all the time, it is probably wise to lock the doors and carry some type of protection.

With high-speed broadband service, your Internet connection is always on, meaning as long as your broadband modem is connected to your home network and it is powered on, your home network and all the computers on it have a connection to the Internet. You are no longer just visiting the bad side of town; with broadband, you are now living there.

Unchecked, hackers, bored or mischievous neighbors (or their kids), or just other people with too much time on their hands can try to access your home network through your broadband connection from anywhere in the world. Broadband also provides hackers with high-speed connections to do a lot more hacking. Once hacked, you cannot undo what you may lose, such as personal data, access to financial accounts, and so on. So, the only real option is to prevent yourself from being hacked in the first place.

Firewalls provide a means to block unwanted visitors from gaining access to your home network, the computers on it, and the information those computers contain.

Why Do I Need Firewalls?

Why would someone want to access your home network? Well, for a lot of reasons, ranging from simple theft of the information on your computers to hijacking your computers and using the anonymity they can provide to conduct other illegal activities. It is impossible to list here all the examples, but let's consider two common ones.

First, most people regularly store information, such as e-mail, spreadsheets, and even passwords to online accounts (eBay and PayPal, for example) on their computers. Figure 1-1 shows how a hacker can launch what is called a brute-force attack to gain access to one of your computers. Tools to perform such attacks, which are easily available on the Internet, use dictionary files to repeatedly attempt to guess your password to remotely log in to your computer or to access a shared drive.

Figure 1-1   Sample Brute-Force Password Attack

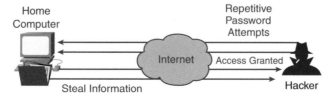

If left unchecked, hackers can attempt thousands of times until they succeed. When into the computer, they can simply help themselves to whatever information you have stored there.

In the second example, it is not the information itself on the computers the hacker is interested in, but enlisting your computer (probably along with hundreds or thousands of others) into what is called a *bot army*. Bot armies are when a hacker has taken over control of many computers and then uses the computers for illicit means, such as to attack other computers or corporate websites. Figure 1-2 shows an example of using a bot army to conduct a *distributed denial-of-service* (DDoS) attack.

Figure 1-2   Sample DDoS Attack

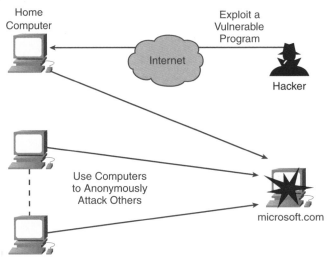

By exploiting a security flaw in the computer's operating system, hackers can install a small program to take remote control of your computer. After doing so on hundreds or thousands of other computers, hackers can then go after their target with a DDoS attack by instructing all the remote-control computers in the bot army to start sending web page requests to a website such as Microsoft.com and repeat the requests as often as possible. If successful, the tens of thousands of requests can cause a spike in the web server and possibly cause it to fail because of overloading. If they cannot cause the server to fail entirely, it might be possible to disrupt or slow down the service to legitimate folks who are trying to access the website.

This is called a DDoS attack. If the attack were conducted from a single computer, the website owners might be able to recognize a pattern and simply block that computer from making future requests. However, if the attack is coming from thousands of people's home computers, how can the website owner distinguish legitimate requests from an attack? That's the point of a bot army: scale, anonymity, and stealth.

We do not pretend to have the answers to why people do such things. Quite frankly, many of them are highly intelligent folks, who for whatever reason have decided to run against society's grain. Regardless of why, they do it; so, it is important for you not to be a victim.

How Firewalls Work

Firewalls can protect your home network by monitoring your broadband Internet connection and only permitting legitimate traffic (the data packets coming in and out of your network) to reach its destination. Firewalls come in two basic types: *stateful packet inspection* (SPI) firewalls and personal software firewalls (sometimes referred to as packet-filtering firewalls). The following two sections discuss and compare the different types.

Stateful Packet Inspection Firewalls

Let's examine what an SPI firewall is. Packets are messages containing pieces of data used to communicate between your computers or with the Internet. Inspecting those packets means we look at each one and check whether it is a legitimate message. Stateful means that not only are we going to check each message itself, but check that the message is sent or received at the right time in the conversation.

For example, suppose two people, Sally and Rick, are talking and the conversation goes something like this:

> Rick: "Hi Sally."
> Sally: "Hi Rick."
> Rick: "'sup girl?"
> Sally: "Hi Rick."
> Rick: "Did you hear me Sally? I asked, 'sup girl?"
> Sally: "Hi Rick."

What can we learn? Well, after Rick asks, "'sup girl?" the first time, we expected Sally to say something witty, such as, "The sky and your cholesterol." Instead, she repeats, "Hi Rick." That sounds fishy because it is not what we expected Sally to say at that point in the conversation. Even fishier is she repeats it a third time. So we can conclude either that Sally has been taken over by an alien or replaced by a robot. Either way, we are probably done talking to her and politely smile as we walk away.

SPI works in a similar way. Figure 1-3 shows an example of an SPI firewall on a broadband Internet connection.

Figure 1-3   How SPI Firewalls Work

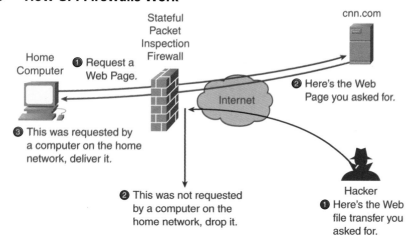

As shown in the green series of events in Figure 1-3, as a computer on the home network originates a request for a web page, the SPI firewall inspects the request as it passes and makes note of the request. Next, when the website responds with the web page, the SPI firewall inspects the response. It looks in its memory and realizes that, yes, this web page response was because of the computer on the home network asking for it, and the SPI firewall allows the web page through to the home network.

If a hacker or some other computer attempts to send a message to a computer in the home network, such as in the red series of events in Figure 1-3, the SPI firewall inspects the message again. This time, however, the firewall cannot make the connection between the message and a request from the home network because such a request did not occur. So, the firewall blocks the message.

Pretty neat. SPI firewalls are an effective way to keep out unwanted intrusions into your home network. They do not solve everything; after all, hackers are crafty and figure out ways around just about everything. However, SPI firewalls can at least dramatically increase the level of protection you have to start with.

If only we had SPI firewalls for our phone lines to keep telemarketers from calling us unless we called them first.

Personal Software Firewalls

Personal software firewalls have a slightly different role in your home network security. Whereas SPI firewalls are usually meant as a barrier to what can come *from* the Internet, personal software firewalls act as a barrier to what can go *to* the Internet from your computers.

Figure 1-4 shows an example of a personal software firewall. A web browser, such as Internet Explorer, attempts to send a web page request to the Internet. The personal software firewall is set up to allow access for this program, so the request is allowed, and the web page is retrieved.

Figure 1-4   How Personal Software Firewalls Work

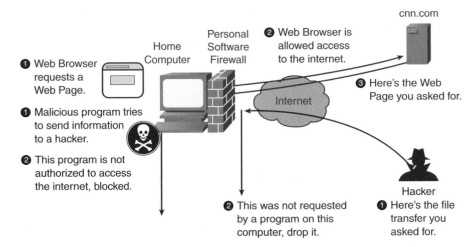

Suppose, however, that despite your best attempts, your computer becomes infected with a Trojan horse virus program (see Chapter 3, "Tip 3: Use Antivirus Protection," for more information on viruses). Now the little devil attempts to send information back to the hackers who planted it, as depicted in Figure 1-4. This time, however, the personal software firewall intercepts the access attempt because that program is not set up to be permitted access to the Internet. The request is denied, and the hacker does not receive the information from your computer.

Just to confuse things a little, many personal software firewall programs also contain an SPI firewall for both outbound and inbound protection, as depicted in the lower right of Figure 1-4. Sweet.

Putting Firewalls to Work

Now that you understand a bit about how they work, let's take a look at where you should place firewalls in your home network and then go ahead and turn them on. Keep in mind that even if your device comes with a built-in firewall, it may not be turned on by default.

Figure 1-5 shows where firewalls are recommended in your home network. First, it is absolutely essential to place an SPI firewall between your high-speed broadband service and your home network. Fortunately, most home network routers now ship with a built-in SPI firewall, so it might require just turning it on.

Figure 1-5   Where You Need Firewalls in Your Home Network

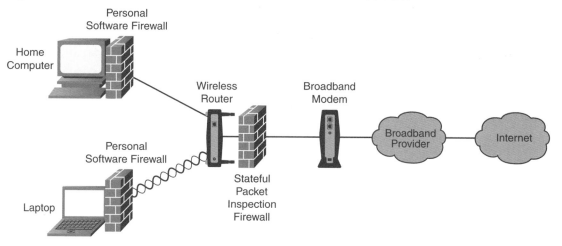

Next, you need to install personal software firewalls on each of the computers in your network. As mentioned before, if the personal software firewalls on the computers also contain SPI firewall functions, all the better.

Each type of firewall presents several options. The next few sections explore the options, help you decide what is best for you, and help you install and turn them on.

Putting a Firewall Between You and the Internet

As previously mentioned, you first need to place an SPI firewall between your home network and the Internet. You can do so either by installing a dedicated firewall device between your broadband cable or *digital subscriber line* (DSL) modem and your home network router or, if available, just turning the SPI firewall on inside your home router.

VERY IMPORTANT: **We *highly* recommend you install a home network router between your high-speed broadband connection and the computers in your home. The router itself provides critical security functions such as *Network Address Translation* (NAT), providing a level of defense for your home network. For more information, see *Home Networking Simplified*, which contains a complete discussion on the importance of home routers.**

To make it really easy, many home network routers are being shipped with built-in SPI firewalls, so all you have to do is turn it on. Nearly all new Linksys wired and wireless routers are equipped with a built-in SPI firewall. If your home router already has an SPI firewall, turn it on and you are done. If it does not, you need to make a decision about how to proceed.

VERY IMPORTANT: **Make sure whatever you buy has an SPI firewall. Some products claim to include a firewall, but the term *firewall* can be interpreted several ways. Look on the box or ask a store professional to make sure what you are buying has SPI.**

Routers with a Built-In Firewall

Because a home network router already has to handle all the messages between your computers and the Internet, it is also a convenient place to put an SPI firewall.

To activate it, you need to access the router's administration function, usually with an Internet browser or a client on one of your computers. Figure 1-6 shows turning on the SPI firewall in a Linksys wireless router (model WRT54GS in this example).

The steps for turning on your firewall are as follows:

Step 1   Access the router's administration function. For Linksys routers, use Internet Explorer and enter the router's IP address in your home network (usually 192.168.1.1).

Step 2   When prompted, enter the administrator user ID and password.

Step 3   Click the **Security** tab.

Step 4   Click **Enable** for the firewall function.

Step 5   Also checkmark the optional additional protection functions, including **Block Anonymous Internet Requests, Filter Multicast, Filter Internet NAT Redirection**, and **Filter IDENT(Port 113)**. These are to detect and block several specific known hacking attacks.

Step 6   Click **Save Settings**.

Figure 1-6   Turning On a Home Router-Based Firewall

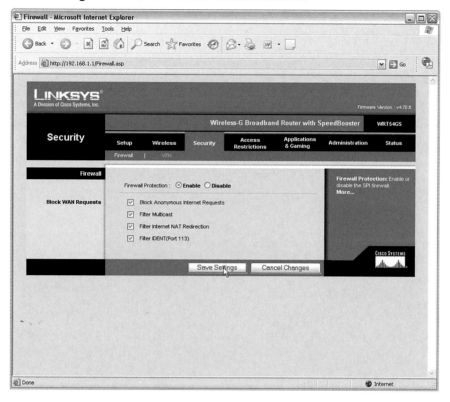

That's it. Now your SPI firewall is running and protecting your home network from the Internet. You have just taken an extremely important step to protecting your home network.

You might ask, "How do I know it is working?" Great question. See you are already learning to become suspicious and think security. Read on and we will give you some tips to make sure what you think you have working really is protecting you like you think.

Dedicated Firewall Devices

If your home network router does not offer a built-in SPI firewall, you must decide whether to replace your home network router with one that does or purchase and install a dedicated firewall device. A *dedicated firewall device* is essentially a box that you place between your broadband modem and your home router that acts 100 percent of the time as a firewall. It provides no other networking functions.

In corporate security circles, dedicated firewalls are preferred because security-minded folks argue that if you keep the software in the box simple, it will have fewer security holes, and as soon as you start adding other functions to it, you add complexity and open up the possibility for holes.

For your home network, dedicated firewalls are becoming extremely rare because it is much more economical and space efficient to have the home router provide the function.

If you decide to go with a dedicated firewall, be aware that each one differs according to the manu-facturer. We suggest following the manufacturer's installation instructions.

VERY IMPORTANT: **If you already have an older home network router installed that does not have an SPI firewall—for example, an older Wireless-B standard router—you might want to kill two birds and consider upgrading to a faster Wireless-G or Wireless-N router and at the same time get the built-in SPI firewall. Chances are you can make both upgrades for the same or less than buying a dedicated firewall device to add to an existing older router.**

Enabling Personal Firewalls on Your Computers

Now that the SPI firewall is protecting the edge of your home network, it's time to turn your atten-tion to the computers on the home network. Each computer needs to have a personal software fire-wall installed. Unlike SPI firewalls, which usually come in physical devices, personal firewalls gener-ally come in the form of software you install on the computer you want to protect.

Here again you have a choice of several options. The first option is Windows XP Service Pack 2 (SP2) and later offers a built-in software firewall. The second option is Zone Labs, which offers its basic ZoneAlarm software firewall for free. Finally, several software firewall programs are available for purchase.

Which you choose depends on your needs, but we try to highlight the advantages and disadvantages of each in the sections that follow.

Windows XP Built-In Firewall

Starting with Windows XP SP2, Windows offers a built-in personal firewall. If you have XP, but do not already have XP SP2 installed, you can obtain it here:

http://www.microsoft.com/windowsxp/sp2/default.mspx

If you have an older version of Windows (including 98SE, ME, or 2000), you are out of luck until you upgrade to XP. See the next sections for other personal software firewall options.

The Windows XP firewall is a basic firewall with program access control (blocking computer to Internet) and SPI (blocking Internet to computer). It is a no-frills approach, but the price is right.

Figures 1-7 and 1-8 show how to enable the Windows XP built-in firewall.

Figure 1-7   Windows XP Security Center

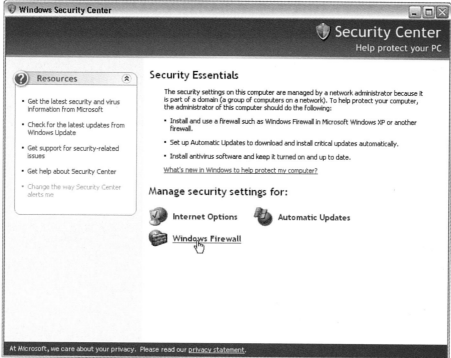

The following are the steps to enable the Windows XP built-in firewall:

Step 1   Click **Start > Control Panel > Security Center**. The main Security Center dialog will display, as shown in Figure 1-7.

VERY IMPORTANT: **If your firewall service was not already running, you will get a popup dialog window with the message "Windows Firewall settings cannot be displayed because the associated service is not running. Do you want to start the Windows Firewall/Internet Connection Sharing (ICS) service?"**

Step 2   Click **Windows Firewall**. You will see the dialog shown in Figure 1-8.

Figure 1-8   Enabling the Built-In Firewall in Windows XP

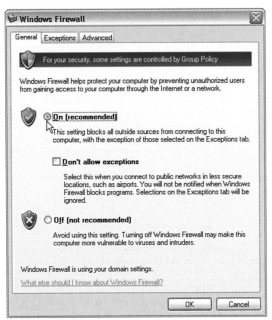

Step 3   Enable the **On (recommended)** button and click **OK** to save the setting.

The Windows XP built-in firewall is now enabled. There are not a lot of other things to configure, and the granularity of control you have is somewhat limited. But, all in all, it is an easy and cost-effective way to enable a personal software firewall on each of your computers. If you want a turn-it-on-and-forget-it firewall and you are running XP, this is a good option.

VERY IMPORTANT: Having the firewall program log interesting events (meaning when it detects unusual activity and takes an action such as dropping the packet) can prove useful for debugging. To enable logging with Windows Firewall, go to the Windows Security Center, click Windows Firewall, and go to the Advanced tab. In the Security Logging section, click Settings and then checkmark what you want to log and choose a location for the log file. To view the log, you must use Notepad to browse the file.

ZoneAlarm Personal Software Firewall

Another relatively easy and cost-effective option for a personal software firewall is ZoneAlarm. Zone Labs offers several versions of its firewall program, including a basic firewall program that is free and a couple more sophisticated versions for purchase.

Let's look at the free version here. The for-purchase version is discussed in the next section. The free ZoneAlarm firewall is a fully functional, pretty good firewall program that includes the functionality you need to protect the computers in your home network. ZoneAlarm is somewhat more configurable than the Windows XP built-in firewall and provides more visibility into what is being blocked or allowed. This could be needed if you run into issues where certain programs you want to have access are being blocked for some reason. With ZoneAlarm, you can see what is being blocked and easily adjust the settings.

VERY IMPORTANT: Typically, only one personal software firewall program can be installed and active on a computer at a time. You generally cannot, for example, run both Windows XP Firewall and ZoneAlarm. Additional firewall programs do not offer any additional protection, and it could lead to complex problems. Pick one, not several. ZoneAlarm in particular disables Windows Firewall when it is installed to avoid such conflicts.

ZoneAlarm is available for download here:

http://www.zonelabs.com

Go to the download area and download the version that is just called ZoneAlarm for the free version.

The following covers some brief installation and setup steps that refer to Figures 1-9 and 1-10.

Step 1 Download and install ZoneAlarm on your computer. You will need to then restart the computer to complete the install.

Step 2 The main ZoneAlarm control dialog is shown in Figure 1-9. If you do not see it on your computer, double-click the yellow and red **ZA** icon that should be in your running tasks at the bottom right of your screen.

Figure 1-9   ZoneAlarm Personal Software Firewall

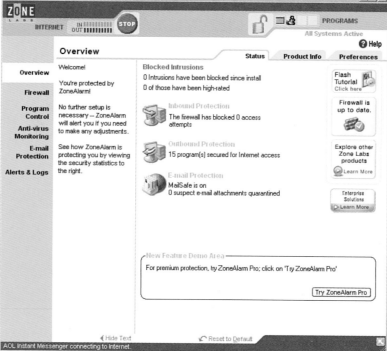

Step 3   ZoneAlarm learns which programs you want to allow or block access to the Internet. When a program attempts access, you will see a popup box as in Figure 1-10.

Figure 1-10   ZoneAlarm Requesting Internet Access for a New Program

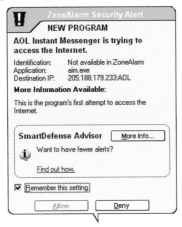

Step 4   Decide whether you want the program to have access. If yes, click the **Allow** button; if not, click **Deny.**

Step 5   Check the **Remember this setting** box prior to clicking **Allow** or **Deny** if you want ZoneAlarm to grant or deny access to this program automatically in the future.

Step 6   If you are not sure whether you want to allow or deny access, perhaps because you do not recognize the program, you can click on **More Info** to seek advice from Zone Labs.

The ZoneAlarm firewall is now enabled. It is a good idea at this point to try to use the programs you normally use, especially those that access the Internet, including Outlook Express (or the alternate e-mail program you use), instant messaging, Internet Explorer (or the alternate browser you use), and so on. Each time a new program tries to access the Internet, ZoneAlarm will prompt you to grant or deny access.

In general, ZoneAlarm initially blocks everything that automatically attempts to access the Internet, including things such as updates to your antivirus programs, which, of course, you want. You can usually read the popup warning and figure it out; if you are not sure what ZoneAlarm is attempting to block, choose the block function and then check the programs you use most often to make sure they are still operating correctly.

If one or more of the programs you used to use no longer works, or if a new program you install does not work properly, you might want to check the access settings in ZoneAlarm to make sure they are not incorrectly set:

Step 1   Double-click the **ZA** icon on your taskbar, or click **Start > Programs > Zone Labs > Zone Labs Security** to launch the ZoneAlarm control dialog. You will see the main Security Center dialog shown previously in Figure 1-9.

Step 2 Click **Program Control** on the left side of the dialog, and click the **Programs** tab at the top. You will see the dialog shown in Figure 1-11.

Figure 1-11   Checking Program Access Settings in ZoneAlarm

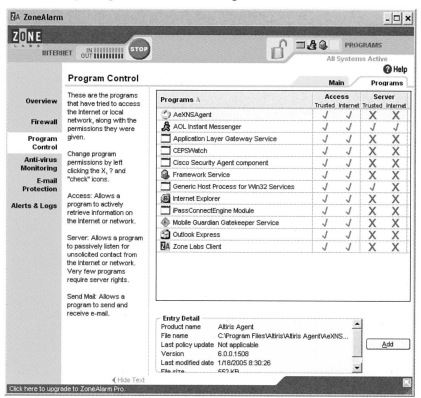

Step 3 Find the program in the list you are trying to use and verify its access control settings. For example, you can see in this case that AOL Instant Messenger has green check-marks next to it, meaning that it is always granted access. Red Xs mean the program is always blocked. Blue question marks indicate that there is no permanent setting and ZoneAlarm will prompt you each time the program runs.

Step 4 To change the access setting, right-click the green check or red X beside the program and select the new setting.

VERY IMPORTANT: You will notice two sets of columns in the Program Control dialog: Access and Server. Access permissions apply to programs on your computer that need access to the Internet. In general, all programs that you want to allow to access the Internet need a minimum of Access permission. Server permission is an additional authorization needed by some programs that legitimately send unsolicited traffic to your computer, such as some e-mail and IM programs. Try allowing Access permissions first; if the program you are using still is not working correctly, try setting the Server permissions to Allow (green checks), too.

In summary, ZoneAlarm firewall is another relatively easy and cost-effective method for enabling a personal software firewall on each of your computers. If you want a firewall program that offers a bit more control and visibility, ZoneAlarm is a good option. If you are not running Windows XP and have no intention to upgrade, again ZoneAlarm is a good option for you.

VERY IMPORTANT: **Having the firewall program log interesting events (meaning when it detects unusual activity and takes an action such as dropping the packet) can prove useful for debugging. Logging is enabled in ZoneAlarm by default. To view the log, bring up the ZoneAlarm main control dialog, click Alerts & Logs, and click the Log Viewer tab.**

Personal Software Firewalls for Purchase

A third option for personal software firewall programs is to purchase one. You may ask, "Why buy one when there are two free options?" Two reasons. First, you get what you pay for, meaning the for-purchase firewall programs are typically going to be kept much more current and have features added to them (not to say that Windows XP Firewall or ZoneAlarm will not).

Second, when you purchase an antivirus software program (notice we said *when*, not if), you have the option of paying a little more money for an entire security bundle. We cover antivirus programs in Chapter 3. Security bundles are offered by the major security software vendors and include a whole suite of protection, including antivirus, firewall, spyware/adware blocking, parental control, antispam, and so on.

We recommend checking out the security bundles from the leading security software vendors in Table 1-1.

Table 1-1   Leading Security Software Bundle Vendors

Security Bundle Provider	Internet Address
McAfee Internet Security Suite	http://www.mcafee.com
Symantec Norton Internet Security 200x	http://www.symantec.com
Trend Micro PC-cillin Internet Security	http://www.trendmicro.com
ZoneAlarm Security Suite	http://www.zonelabs.com

This book lacks space to show them all. Just to give you a feel for how the security packages look, however, the following discussion covers two of them. Keep in mind that you only need one of these firewall programs for your home network; adding a second will only disable the previously loaded firewall programs.

Figure 1-12 shows the main control panel for Symantec's product, Norton Internet Security 200x. You can see that the Personal Firewall component that came included in the bundle is enabled.

Figure 1-12   Symantec Norton Internet Security 200x

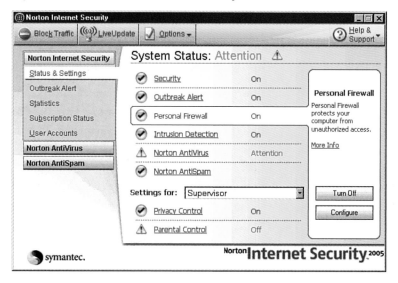

Figure 1-13 shows the main control panel for McAfee's product, Internet Security Suite. Once again, you can see that the Personal Firewall component that came included in the bundle is enabled.

Figure 1-13   McAfee Internet Security Suite

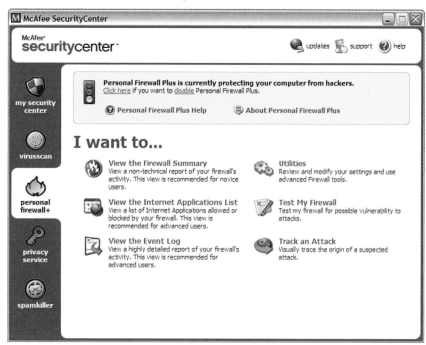

Both of these personal software firewalls operate similarly to ZoneAlarm. Each learns as new programs attempt to access the Internet, and you specify whether to grant or deny access. Both are also configurable and allow for relatively easy control and visibility.

If you decide to purchase a security bundle, the included personal firewall component is a good option. Also, if you need a fully functional firewall program with all the bells and whistles, one of these for-purchase programs is a good option for you. You should also check your Internet service provider's security pages. They often offer bundles and good advice on firewalls and bundled security services.

VERY IMPORTANT: **We highly recommended that you set up personal software firewall programs to automatically start when Windows starts. Having to remember to start the firewall program manually is going to be a pain and hit or miss if you remember to trigger it or not.**

Test Driving Your New Protection

After your new firewall protection is up and running (on both your router and your computers), and when you are comfortable that your programs are still working, it is worth a couple minutes to perform a quick test using an online tool to determine whether the firewalls are doing their job.

You can run a quick test using the port-scanning utility provided by a collection of broadband providers. You can access this here:

http://www.dslreports.com/scan

Click **Probe**, and when it finishes click **Results**. This utility attempts to get responses from your home network, which your SPI firewall should now block. Figure 1-14 shows a sample scan.

You should see all green indicators (not red or yellow), which means that your network is protected. Suggestions are offered if weaknesses in the network security are identified.

Another similar test is provided online by a group opposed to hacking, called Hacker Watch. You can find their test here:

http://www.hackerwatch.org/probe/

Click **Port Scan** to start the test. This utility attempts to get responses from your home network, which your SPI firewall should now block. Figure 1-15 shows a sample result from this test.

Figure 1-14   Testing Security with a Port Scan

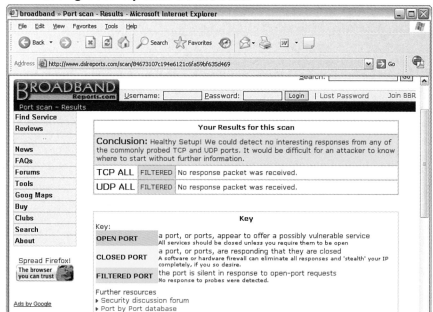

Figure 1-15   Another Test for Evaluating Security

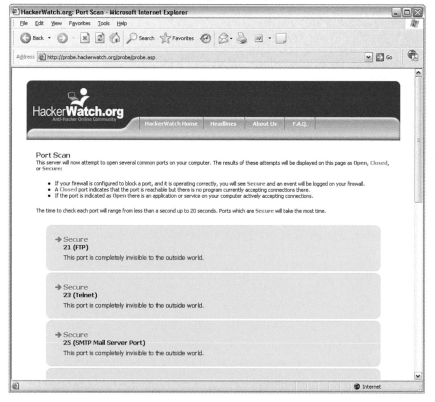

When the test completes, you should again see green indicators, telling you the attempts to send messages into your home network from the Internet were appropriately blocked by your SPI firewall. If security weaknesses exist, some suggestions are made as to how to solve them.

Several other similar security scans are available online, such as the following:

http://www.pcflank.com/test.htm

http://scan.sygate.com

Both of these programs (and several others) all work great. There is really no need to try them all out (but there's nothing wrong with doing that). Just pick one that appeals to you and go with it.

What to Do If You Think You've Been Hacked

Despite our best attempts, stuff happens. One of the most common ways you can get hacked today is by inadvertently unleashing a virus on your computer (see Chapter 3). Just opening an e-mail with a malicious program attached can wreak havoc on your computer, including setting up a Trojan horse program, whereby a hacker can take control of your computer.

Another less-invasive, but no-less-annoying intrusion, is spyware and adware (see Chapter 5, "Tip 5: Lock Out Spyware and Adware"). By installing a "free" program from the "who knows what" website, you can unleash an adware program on your computer that can annoy you with constant popup advertisements, or worse, start transmitting your Internet browsing habits over the Internet to someplace that wants to target you for direct marketing, or even log and report all your keystrokes (including passwords).

Sometimes, no easy way exists to tell whether you have been hijacked or infected. Sometimes, however, there are good ways to tell. One such way is to become familiar with which programs are installed on your computer. If you see a new program appear that you did not install or cause to install, it might be a malicious program.

You can take two steps to address the problem: Block the program's access in the personal software firewall, and uninstall it. Make sure it is malicious before you take action.

Go to the program control screen in your personal software firewall program. For this example, we use ZoneAlarm. As shown in Figure 1-16, access the **Program Control** screen and select the **Programs** tab. Click the program in question (in this example, **GAIN Application**).

Down at the bottom of the window, you can see the filename of the program (in this case, GMT.exe). Doing a quick search online, we can find out that this is a common adware application from GAIN Publishing.

To block it, just right-click the program and select the red X. Now the program is blocked from accessing the Internet.

Blocking the program does nothing to solve the root cause of the problem, meaning the program is still sitting there running on your computer. Adware, and in general any needless program, can slow down performance of your computer dramatically. So, it is usually best to get rid of it.

Figure 1-16   Using ZoneAlarm to Block a Program

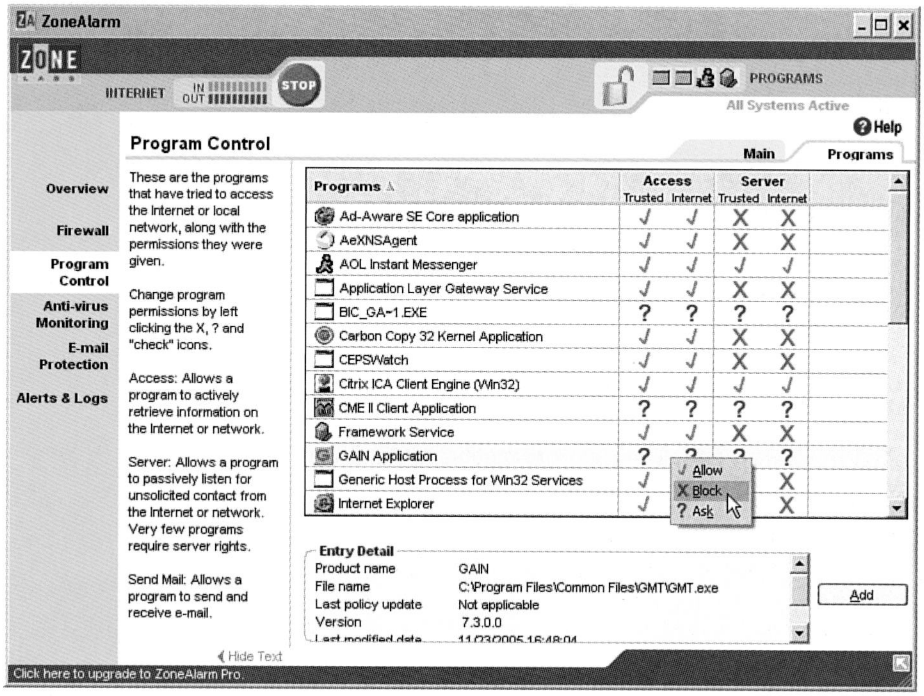

To do so, click **Start > Control Panel > Add/Remove Programs**. As shown in Figure 1-17, click the program you want to remove, and then click **Change/Remove**.

Figure 1-17   Uninstalling an Unwanted Program

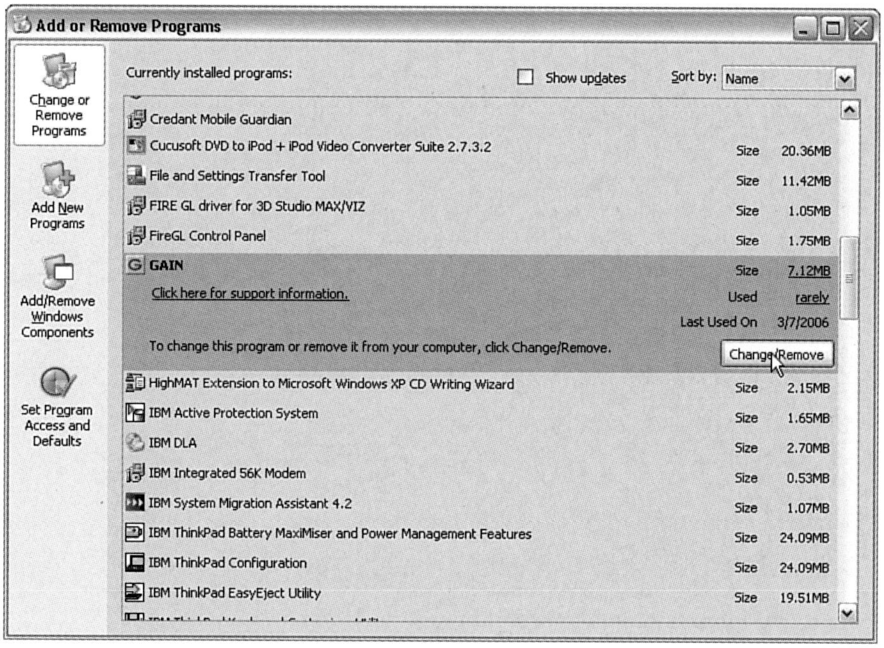

The adware program will be uninstalled. You can then either leave the access rule in ZoneAlarm (recommended) or delete it. If you leave it blocked and the same adware program should inadvertently be installed again, its access to the Internet will be blocked from the start. However, it does tend to produce some clutter in the program list.

In general, it is good practice to become familiar with the programs in the Windows Add/Remove Programs list and the Program Control list in your personal software firewall. That way, when a new entry unexpectedly appears, you can recognize it.

Sometimes, Firewalls Block the Good Stuff

Although firewalls are intended to always block the bad stuff, while letting the good stuff through, it is not always that easy. Sometimes as a side effect of having a firewall, a program you want to access the Internet does not function properly.

The best approach if you suspect the firewall is causing the problem is to temporarily turn off the firewall and determine whether the program now functions. If it does, turn the firewall back on and adjust the access settings for the program. Peer-to-peer-sharing and file-transfer/FTP programs are the most common for this type of problem.

VERY IMPORTANT: **Always remember to turn the firewall back on if you temporarily disable it to debug program access control issues.**

Summary

Firewalls do not solve every home network security issue. They are a critical step for security, but they need to be complemented with the other steps in this book (including antivirus and antispyware/adware).

Also, do not expect a firewall to catch every hack or intrusion attempt. Firewalls are pretty good at blocking today's known hacks. However, crafty folks as the hackers are, they can find new ways around firewalls.

View having appropriate firewalls in your home network as significantly raising the barrier against intruders so that they move on to easier targets.

Where to Go for More Information

To find more information about firewalls, try these websites:

http://www.microsoft.com/technet/security/topics/networksecurity/firewall.mspx

http://www.firewallguide.com/

http://www.howstuffworks.com/firewall.htm

If you want something more technical, we recommend the following site:

http://www.faqs.org/faqs/firewalls-faq/

CHAPTER 2

Tip 2: Secure Your Wireless Network

Threat Type: Access based

Examples of Threats:

- Passers-by getting free Internet access
- Hackers getting access to your computer files
- Hackers "listening" for passwords and other private information

Our Tips:

- Turn off SSID broadcast.
- Use WEP or WPA encryption.
- Change the default password on your router.
- Turn off the ad-hoc networking function.
- Make sure your NIC does not unintentionally roam to someone else's wireless router.

It is pretty likely that you are currently (or will soon be) using a wireless networking device in your home. Wireless is great for all the flexibility it affords when it comes to setting up a home network, and it is cool when you want to surf the web or check e-mail when you are on the deck, or couch... or toilet (like you've never done it).

Wireless is affordable, flexible, and easy to install, and in general we highly recommend it. The problem is that to make it easy to install the manufacturers turn off most if not all the security features so that it connects easily out of the box. In fairness, most of the manufacturers we have looked at do have quick-start guides that show how to enable security, but as we demonstrate in this chapter many people just don't bother. This could be an expensive mistake if you consider what it costs to repair your credit history.

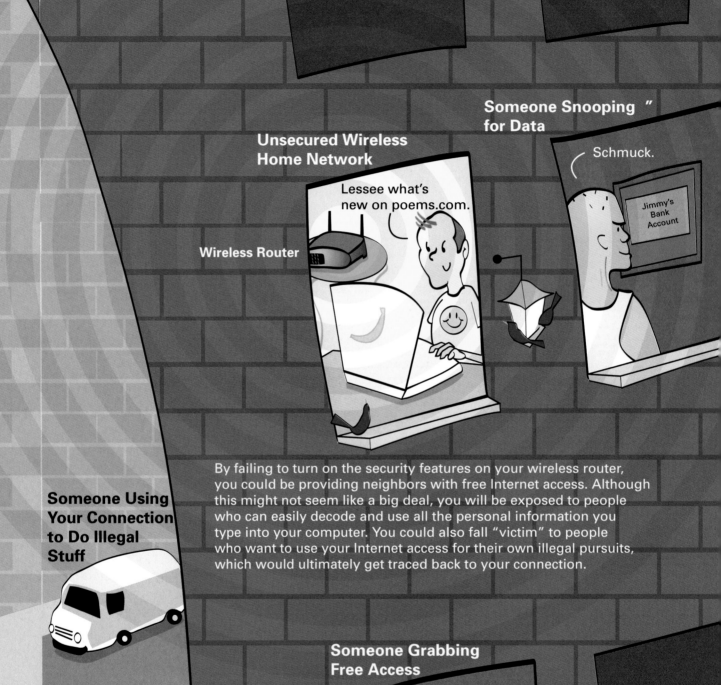

Why Should I Care About Wireless Network Security?

Access to a wired network is easy to control because people have to be physically inside your house to plug a computer into the router. With a wireless network, people just have to be in the proximity of your house. Physical barriers such as windows and doors do not control access in this case, so we have to take other steps to block intruders.

The security issue with a wireless network stems from the fact that the signal is omnidirectional. Unlike a wired network, where signals are fairly well contained, the wireless signal goes everywhere in all directions (including up and down for those of you in multistory buildings) for 300 feet or more. Anyone who wants to gain access to your signal need only put a receiver (a computer with a wireless card) inside the signal range.

VERY IMPORTANT: Why would someone want to access your wireless network? Well, there are lots of reasons. One of your neighbors could "leech" onto your network just to receive free Internet access. Although irritating, this is not all that harmful in itself, if all they are doing is browsing the Internet on your dollar. However, "war drivers" (people who drive around looking for unsecured wireless connections) or professional hackers could use the access to obtain your personal information. For example, eavesdropping while you are conducting an online purchase could expose your credit card information. They could also access the computers on your network.

One of the most unusual illicit uses of unsecured home wireless networks also offers perhaps the strongest reason yet to secure your wireless network. Recently, several instances have surfaced in which people conducting illegal activities used unsecured home networks for the anonymity that they can provide. One fellow parked in a neighborhood, easily gained access to an unprotected home wireless network and downloaded huge amounts of illegal child pornography. He was caught and arrested, but because of a traffic violation, not the downloading. (The police noticed the pictures on the computer after they pulled him over.) If someone commits illegal activity in this manner, it can easily be traced to your broadband subscription, and you could end up having to explain to the authorities (and your family) that it was not you or other family members conducting the illegal activity.

We are always amazed when we drive through a neighborhood and check how people have deployed their wireless networks. On one drive recently, we easily found 114 wireless routers, only 45 (roughly 40 percent) of which were protected in any fashion. From such a scan, potential intruders can easily obtain a survey of the available wireless networks, their *service set identifiers* (SSIDs), channel numbers, and most important, which networks have been secured and which have been left wide open (roughly 60 percent). In Figure 2-1, the networks with a circle and a padlock inside indicate that they are at least using encryption. The circles without a padlock are wide open. Anyone can sit on the street near these houses (or businesses), associate to the access point, and access the Internet or try to break into the rest of the home network. Tools that perform these kinds of searches are free and easy to find and use.

Figure 2-1   Example of Scanning for Wireless Networks in a Neighborhood

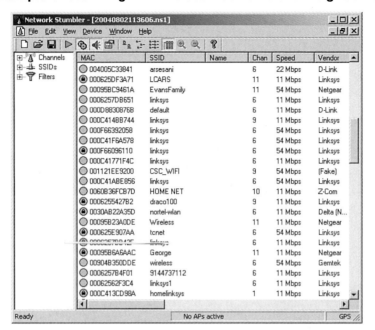

Several of the unsecured sites shown in Figure 2-1 are in the same condition that your wireless router is in when you take it out of the box. In other words, these people took their router out of the box, hooked it up, and started using it without enabling wireless security. It is great for getting up and running fast, but if you do not take a few minutes to secure your router (and it really only takes a few minutes), you could be asking for trouble.

What Do I Do About Wireless Security?

You can take three really simple steps to dramatically increase the security of your wireless network. It is not foolproof wireless security, but it will keep you from being an easy target and it will keep most of the riff raff out.

As Figure 2-1 shows, there are plenty of easy targets out there, so all you need to worry about in most cases is the curious neighbor or someone specifically looking to access a network with no protection at all. The steps in this chapter will not keep out a really serious hacker; if you have reason to worry about a hacker specifically targeting you (as opposed to someone hacking at random), however, you can hire a security specialist, or better yet, just do not use wireless. For the vast majority of you, though, read on.

Figure 2-2 shows varying degrees of wireless home network security and the vulnerabilities related to the networks.

Figure 2-2   Wireless Security Examples

Wireless Settings
Enabled SSID Broadcast
Default SSID (e.g., linksys)
No Encryption
No MAC Filtering

Wireless Settings
Disable SSID Broadcast
Changed SSID (e.g., fluffycat)
No Encryption
No MAC Filtering

Wireless Settings
Disable SSID Broadcast
Random SSID (e.g., kr90oLMZ)
128-Bit WEP Encryption
No MAC Filtering

Wireless Settings
Disable SSID Broadcast
Random SSID (e.g., Fh560S0eeXt)
WPA2 Encryption
MAC Filtering

Security Issues
Wireless routers come
from the store this way.
Anyone with a laptop can
get on this network, and
most hotspot programs
will make it easy. Don't do this.

This person is asking for trouble!

Security Issues
This network will keep most
non-hackers off the network, but all
your information (including e-mail
online shopping data) is sent in
cleartext for anyone to see.

This person is still vulnerable.

Security Issues
This network is secure enough
for most people, including
encrypting all data sent and
received. There are more secure
options, but this is the
minimum you should do.

**Secure enough for most
people, but a dedicated hacker
could take you down.**

Security Issues
This network has the most
security possible today and is
equivalent to business-class
security. However, it's more complex
to implement. If you need more
than this, hire a professional.

Very secure.

So what are the four things you need to do?

- Change your router's password.

- Do not advertise your network (turn off SSID broadcast).

- Scramble (encrypt) your wireless signal (use WEP or WPA).

- Do not use ad-hoc networking.

Before we get into the "How to Do It" section, let's take a closer look at the "what" and "why" of wireless network security. Do not worry if this seems a bit complicated; it really is not. The "How to Do It: Securing Your Wireless Network" section walks you through the setup so that these basic security features can be turned on in a fairly painless way. Trust us here: It is a far worse pain to have people get on and take advantage of your network than to implement these steps.

Change Your Password

Pretty much every router on the planet comes with a default password of admin. If you don't change this immediately upon turning on and connecting to your router, you are asking for trouble. You need to open the screen where the password gets changed anyway, so do yourself a favor. Chapter 8, "Tip 8: Create Strong Passwords," explains how to create strong passwords.

Do Not Advertise Your Wireless Network

Every wireless router is given a name that allows clients (wireless-enabled computers) to find and associate to it. This name is called the service set identifier, or SSID. The first thing you can do to greatly improve the security of your wireless network is not to broadcast the SSID.

Most wireless routers have the broadcast SSID setting turned on when you take them out of the box. This feature announces the name of your network to every wireless-capable computer within range. Although this makes it easy for you to connect to your network, it makes it easy for the rest of the neighborhood, too. Turn this feature off (we show you how later in the section "Stop Advertising Your Wireless Network"). In addition, remember that knowing the name of a network (even if the broadcast function is turned off) gives you the power to get on that network, so you should choose a random SSID name. The same rules that apply to any password apply here, too, so take a look at Chapter 8.

Any SSID that is easy for you to remember is probably easy to figure out, so avoid SSIDs that include your name, the word *home,* the word *network,* or anything related to *your name-homewireless-network*. We suggest that you rename the SSID to something personal (but not easily guessed), or use a random combination of numbers and upper- and lowercase letters. Do not worry about having to memorize this; you can just write it down and keep in a drawer or a folder where you can access it later if you need it. Remember, however, that these steps only keep out the nosy neighbors and provide your router with some level of anonymity, but this step does not by itself protect your network.

Scramble Your Signal

Another thing you can do to improve the security of your network is to turn on encryption. If you are unfamiliar with encryption, the concept is pretty simple. Remember being a kid and making up a list like this:

A	B	C	D	E	F	G	H	I	J	K	L	M	N	O	P	Q	R	S	T	U	V	W	X	Y	Z
1	2	3	4	5	6	7	8	9	10	11	12	13	14	15	16	17	18	19	20	21	22	23	24	25	26

Then your friend writes you a note like this:

9

12 15 22 5

12 9 19 1

You pull out your handy-dandy decoder table and translate it to "I love Lisa." Congratulations, you were doing encryption.

We are obviously oversimplifying, but encrypting your wireless network is actually a similar concept. You are going to choose a "key" for your wireless network. That key is known to both the sender and receiver (for example, your computer and the wireless router). Every time you send information between each other, you use the key to encode it, transmit it, and then use the key again to decode the message back to its real information.

In the case of wireless encryption, instead of a single letter to number translation, a mathematical formula is calculated using the original information and the key. The result is a highly encoded piece of information that is difficult to decode without knowing the key. In general, the longer the key, the harder it is to break. Think of an encryption key like a PIN code that has 64 or 128 digits instead of 4. (How the mathematical formulas work are beyond the scope of this book. If you are interested, pick up a book on cryptography.)

In the end, though, what is important is that even if someone intercepts the signal between your computer and your router, if you are using encryption that person will not be able to make heads or tails out of the information.

Several standards are available for wireless network encryption, including the two most common ones:

- **Wired Equivalent Privacy (WEP)**—Provides a simple and fairly effective means for keeping your information private and your network secure from those wishing to access it without your knowledge or approval. WEP is the most widely available encryption standard and is offered with several different key lengths, including 64, 128, 152, and even 256 (bits). You may also see references to 40 and 104, but these are exactly the same as 64 and 128. WEP is good enough to keep any nonhacker from seeing your information but is not a bulletproof encryption method.

- **Wi-Fi Protected Access (WPA)**—A newer and more sophisticated method of encryption. We recommend that you use WPA if it is available on your gear because it provides better protection than WEP. The major difference between WEP and WPA is that with WEP your encryption key remains the same until you change it, whereas WPA changes the key periodically (you don't have to worry about the changes; it is done automatically for you). Changing the key makes it more difficult for others to discover the key, and even if they do the key is only useful for a short time because it will change again. There are two versions of WPA: WPA and WPA2. WPA2 adds a newer encryption algorithm called *Advanced Encryption Standard* (AES), which provides "business-level" security for home networks.

Some home networking products (wireless computers, access cards, and wireless routers) support all the encryption options, whereas others support a smaller subset. This is important because both the computer and router need to be talking with the same encryption method and key to understand each other.

Table 2-1 summarizes the different encryption methods mentioned previously. It is important to note that these encryption methods typically cannot be mixed together on the same network, so pick the highest level of security that all your wireless network devices can support.

Table 2-1   Available Wireless Encryption Methods—Choosing an Encryption Key

Encryption Method	Security	Recommendations
WPA2		Adds a new encryption algorithm (AES) to WPA, which makes it even more secure. Not likely to be available for older devices.
WPA		Adds a degree of security beyond WEP. The secret key is changed periodically to reduce the opportunity for "cracking." Typically available with a software upgrade for older devices.
128-bit WEP (sometimes referred to as 104-bit WEP)		Commonly used and offers a high degree of security. A professional hacker with enough money and time can "crack" the code, but this is reasonably secure for most people.
64-bit WEP (sometimes referred to as 40-bit WEP)		Minimum level of encryption. We recommend 128-bit WEP. However, if you have some older devices, they may only support 64-bit WEP.

So, how do you choose an encryption key? There are two ways, one very simple, one not so simple. The simple way is to use the key generator that is built in to the home networking products. (Linksys products offer this in every wireless card and router they sell.) Essentially, you just create a passphrase (which is like a password), enter it into the *network interface card* (NIC) or router (using the administration tool), and click a **Generate Key** button. Examples are shown later in the "Enable Wireless Encryption" section. The same rules apply to passphrase selection as passwords: Never use names, pets, or words. Make up a random series of 8 to 63 lowercase letters, uppercase letters, and numbers. Do *not* try to spell words or use clever encoded phrases such as weLUVr2Dogs. (Chapter 8 has more on creating strong passwords.) The key generator takes the passphrase and translates it into a series of numbers (0–9) and letters (A–F). Do not worry about understanding the number system, but this is the encryption key. Write down both the passphrase and generated key; we are going to need it several times.

VERY IMPORTANT: **We cannot stress enough that whenever you create something such as an encryption pass code, password, or WEP key, you need to write it down in your notebook. If you lose it, you might have to reset the wireless router to the factory defaults and start over.**

The second way to choose an encryption key is make it up yourself using a random combination of numbers (0–9) and letters (A–F). You must create an exact number of numbers and letters depending on which key length you are trying to create. For example, a 64-bit key has 10 digits, a 128-bit key has 26 digits, and so on. (The admin screen where you set this up specifies the number of characters.) If at all possible, use the built-in key generator from a passphrase. You will pull your hair out trying to create them by hand.

VERY IMPORTANT: **If you have been paying close attention, you might be confused. If each hexadecimal digit in the key is 4 bits, how can a 64-bit key have 10 hexadecimal digits and a 128-bit key have 26 hexadecimal digits? Wouldn't that be 40 and 104 bits, respectively? The answer is that there is also a 24-bit random number that gets added to each key that makes up the other 6 hexadecimal digits in the full key length.**

Oh, and remember if you have guests who want to use your network you will need to give them your passphrase or security key. If you need to, you can always change the key after they leave. You can also have them use a direct (wired) connection into the router, which does not require encryption.

Disable Ad-Hoc Networking

Your wireless-enabled computer has two basic modes of communication: infrastructure and ad-hoc networking. In infrastructure mode, all the computers on the network must communicate through the router. So whether you are talking to the Internet or with another computer on the local network, all your communication traffic goes through the router. This is what most people are and should be doing.

In ad-hoc mode, computers can communicate directly with each other without going through a router or any other device. This is great if, for example, you want to share a file with someone quickly. The bad thing is that if you have this mode enabled, those who know what they are doing can get access to all your files, possibly without you even noticing it. To avoid this, we strongly recommend that you disable this function. If you find yourself in a situation where you need to use this feature (such as visiting a friend's home that only has an ad-hoc network), turn it on for the duration of use and then immediately disable it.

How to Do It: Securing Your Wireless Network

Here is an overview of the steps you'll go through in this section:

- Change the router's default password.
- Stop advertising your wireless network.
- Enable wireless encryption.
- Disable ad-hoc networking.
- Prevent unintentional roaming.

Change the Router's Default Password

As previously mentioned, routers from the same manufacturers all come with the same password. Although it may be easy to keep it the way it is out of the box, it is well worth the 30 seconds it takes to change it.

Here are the configuration steps that you need to do:

Step 1   Access the wireless router using your Internet browser.

Step 2   Click the **Setup** tab.

Step 3   Click the change password option.

Stop Advertising Your Wireless Network

By default, wireless routers are set up to broadcast their SSID to make it easy for wireless cards to learn the wireless network without having to know information in advance. Nice feature, bad security practice. Broadcasting the SSID of our wireless home network is entirely unnecessary. So, the first step to securing our network is to shut it off.

Here's the configuration steps that we need to do:

Step 1   Access the wireless router using your Internet browser. You should be connected via a wired connection because any change you make could break the connection between the router and the computer if you have only a wireless connection at the time.

Step 2   Click the Wireless tab.

Step 3   On the line labeled Wireless SSID Broadcast, checkmark Disable (see Figure 2-3).

Figure 2-3   Disabling the SSID Broadcast

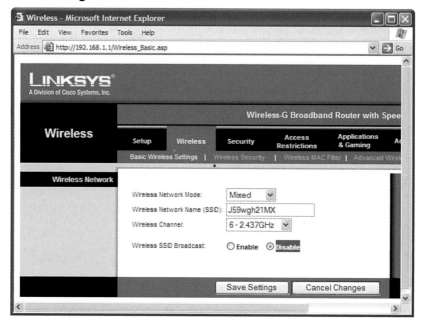

Step 4   While you are on that screen, change the SSID name to something random (write it down). Remember that you also need to change the name on the wireless set screen of each computer you access this network with.

Step 5   Click Save Settings. That's it!

Just by taking these simple steps, you have made your wireless network relatively invisible and fairly anonymous so that people looking for signals will not see a router with your name on it.

VERY IMPORTANT: **As a reminder, *never* use the default SSID that the wireless router is set up with. (For Linksys products this is linksys.) If the SSID is not being broadcast but is easily guessed by intruders, your wireless network is still vulnerable. Change the SSID to something else, such as a random series of uppercase letters, lowercase letters, and numbers. Write it down.**

Enable Wireless Encryption

Even with reduced visibility to your wireless network, a more sophisticated eavesdropper still might be able to learn the SSID and try to obtain access, so you need more security. The next step to securing the wireless network is to turn on encryption. Again, by default, encryption is disabled in wireless router products out of the box. To turn on encryption, we make up a secret key (see the previous section on encryption) that is known only by the wireless router and the wireless NICs in our wireless network (NIC stands for network interface card, which is the wireless-enabled card in your computer that allows connection to a wireless router). To communicate, this secret key must be known; otherwise, the conversation is unintelligible.

In general, both the wireless router and all wireless cards in your network have to be running the same encryption method. However, depending on the age of the wireless product, they may not support all options listed in Table 2-1. The key then is to examine what each device (including the router) supports and use the highest level of encryption that all of them can handle. Meaning, start at the top of the table, if all your devices support WPA2, use it. If even one of the devices you plan to network does not, you either need to replace it with one that does or go down in the table (for example, WPA or 128-bit WEP).

VERY IMPORTANT: **Keep in mind that even 128-bit WEP is pretty good and will defeat "curious neighbors," but it will not keep a real hacker out. WPA2 is approaching the level of wireless network security that large corporations rely on. So, although you do not need to be overly alarmed if your network "only" supports 128-bit WEP, you should consider upgrading to products that support WPA, or better yet WPA2.**

After you choose your method of encryption, you need to implement it on the wireless router and all wireless cards in your network. Each device must be "told" what the super-secret key is to be able to join the conversation.

Enabling WEP Encryption on the Wireless Router

First, let's take an example of implementing 128-bit WEP encryption. We will pick a passphrase of 64Gx3prY19fk2. Now, let's program the wireless router to use this WEP key.

VERY IMPORTANT: **It is good practice to always make any modifications to the settings on your wireless router from a computer that has a wired connection, not a wireless connection. This is especially true when changing the wireless settings, such as WEP encryption. If you make a mistake (a typo for example on the passphrase), you will be unable to reconnect your computers to the router, thus cutting off the limb you are standing on.**

Step 1   As we have done several times, access the wireless router using your Internet browser. Click the **Wireless** tab.

Step 2   Click the **Wireless Security** subtab (see Figure 2-4). On the line labeled Security Mode, select **WEP**.

Figure 2-4   Select WEP as Your Security Mode

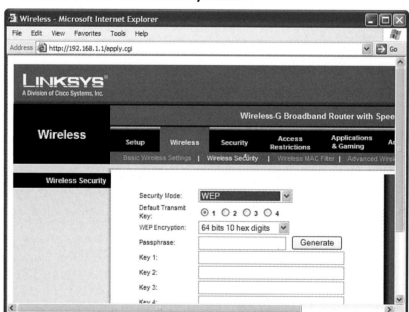

Step 3   On the line labeled WEP Encryption, select **128 bits**. On the line labeled Passphrase, enter the passphrase you made up. In our example, we chose 64Gx3prY19fk2 (see Figure 2-5). Click **Generate**. This translates the passphrase into the actual key to be used. Do not forget to write down the passphrase.

Figure 2-5   Generate the WEP Key

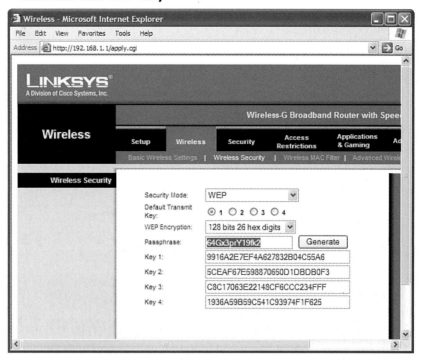

> **Step 4**   Click Save Settings.

Immediately after you click **Save Settings**, any computers that were connected with a wireless card to the wireless router will lose connectivity. This is normal because you have just changed the way they are supposed to communicate with the wireless router, but you have not told them the super-secret password to use yet. Let's do that now for each wireless NIC.

VERY IMPORTANT: **You may notice four keys are listed after you generate the WEP key. In general, you can choose any of the four keys, but most often you can just pick key number one. The other three keys are just alternate keys that you can use if you want to keep the same passphrase but change the actual key. Keep in mind that if you choose a key other than number one, write it down because this is the key you will also need to enter in all the wireless NICs.**

Enabling WEP Encryption on the Wireless NIC

There are a couple different ways to manage the wireless connection in each of your computers. Windows XP offers a built-in function for wireless NIC management. With computers with older versions of Windows (2000, 98SE, and so on) most likely you need to use a wireless management program that comes with the NIC.

The sections that follow show two examples: a Windows 98 desktop computer with a USB-connected wireless card that we set up with the Linksys WLAN utility and a Windows XP laptop that we set up using the XP built-in wireless NIC management function.

Enabling WEP Encryption Using the Linksys Utility

First, let's walk through an example of setting up WEP encryption on a computer running Windows 98SE, using a USB wireless NIC and the Linksys WLAN utility:

Step 1   Launch the Linksys WLAN Monitor by double-clicking the icon on the far right of your Windows taskbar (the example shows a computer running Windows 98/Me/2000).

If you do not see such an icon, try going through **Start > Programs > Instant Wireless > Instant Wireless LAN Monitor**.

Notice there is no connection to the wireless router (the signal bars are not "lit" up). (See Figure 2-6.)

Click the **Profiles** tab.

Figure 2-6   Launch the WLAN Monitor Utility

Step 2   Select the profile for your home wireless network, and click **Edit** (see Figure 2-7).

Figure 2-7   Select and Edit the Wireless Profile

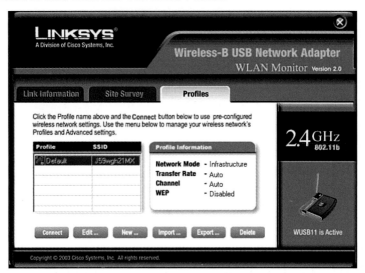

Step 3   No changes are needed to the Network Settings (see Figure 2-8). Click **Next**.

Figure 2-8   Network Settings Stay the Same

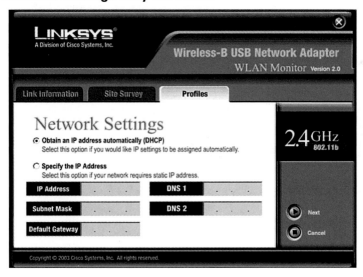

Step 4   No changes are needed to the Network Mode either (see Figure 2-9). Click **Next**.

Figure 2-9   Network Mode Stays the Same

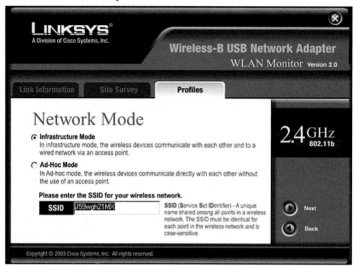

The Security Settings window appears.

Step 5   On the line labeled WEP, select **128-bit**.

On the line labeled Passphrase, enter the passphrase you made up. In our example, we chose 64Gx3prY19fk2 (see Figure 2-10). Leave the WEP Key and TX Key fields alone.

Step 6   Click **Next**.

Figure 2-10   Generate the WEP Key

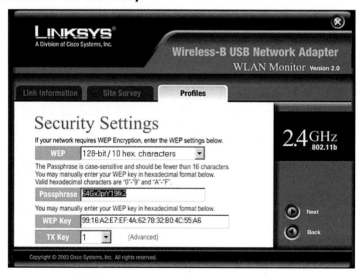

VERY IMPORTANT: Make sure to enter the passphrase exactly as you did on the wireless router. Lowercase *a* is different from uppercase *A*. The two keys (on the router and on the wireless card) must be identical.

Step 7   A confirmation window appears (see Figure 2-11).

Double-check that WEP is set to 128-bit and click **Yes**.

Figure 2-11   Confirm the New Settings

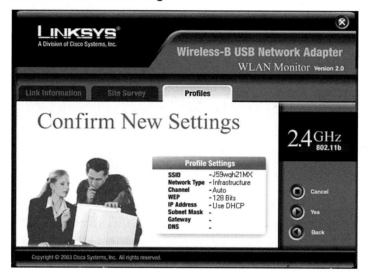

Step 8   Another confirmation window appears (see Figure 2-12). Click **Activate new settings now**.

Figure 2-12   Activate Your New Settings

Step 9   Click the **Link Information** tab. If you entered everything correctly, the Signal Strength and Link Quality should reappear as green bars (see Figure 2-13).

Figure 2-13   Success at Last!

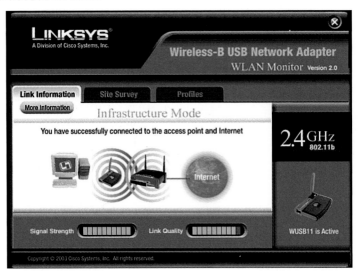

VERY IMPORTANT: **The green bars may or may not be solid the whole way across. It depends on the strength of the wireless signal and how far away you are from the wireless router, much like a cell phone.**

If not, you probably entered something incorrectly. See the "Troubleshooting Tips: Wireless Encryption" sidebar later in this chapter for help.

Enabling WEP Encryption Using Windows XP

Now let's walk through enabling WEP encryption on a built-in wireless NIC on a laptop computer running Windows XP:

Step 1   Select **Start > Control Panel > Network Connections**.

Note the red X on the Wireless Network Connection icon (see Figure 2-14). This is normal and means we have lost communication with the wireless router.

Click the **Wireless Network Connection** icon in the right section of the window, and then click **Change settings of this connection** on the left.

Figure 2-14   Windows XP Network Connections

Step 2   Click the **Wireless Networks** tab (see Figure 2-15).

Figure 2-15   Wireless NIC Settings

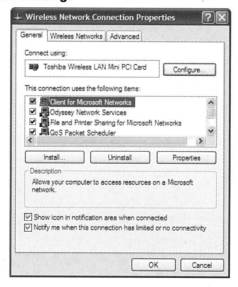

Step 3   In the Preferred networks section, select the entry for your wireless home network and click the **Properties** button (see Figure 2-16).

Figure 2-16   Modify the Wireless Network Properties

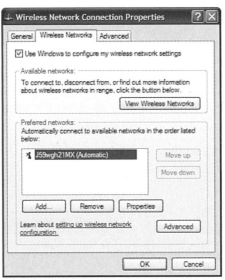

Step 4   Select **WEP** for data encryption (see Figure 2-17).

Figure 2-17   Enable WEP and Enter the WEP Key

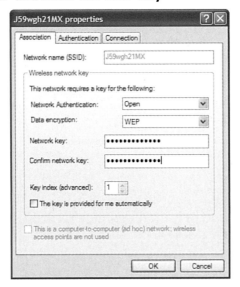

In the box labeled Network key, enter the WEP key you generated using the wireless router. In our example, we chose 64Gx3prY19fk2 as the passphrase, which generated 9916A2E7EF4A627832B04C55A6 as the key. Enter the key, not the passphrase, when using Windows XP to manage your wireless cards.

Everyone repeat in unison: write down the passphrase, write down the key.

VERY IMPORTANT: **Windows XP does not support passphrase WEP key generation. If you have Windows XP and are using it to manage the wireless connection, you must enter the WEP key itself, not the passphrase. You should have the WEP key written down from when you enabled WEP encryption on the wireless router.**

If the "The key is provided for me automatically" box is check marked, uncheck it.

Click **OK**.

Step 5   You should now see the entry in the Preferred Networks section show a connection (as indicated by the icon). (See Figure 2-18.)

Click **OK**.

Figure 2-18   Verify the Wireless Network Profile

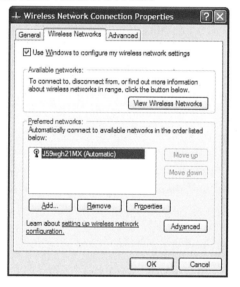

Step 6   Going back to the Network Connections window, the red X should now be gone from the Wireless Network Connection icon (see Figure 2-19). This means that you're all done, and the wireless NIC is now communicating with the wireless router using encryption.

Figure 2-19 Encryption Is Enabled and Working

WPA Encryption Example

To compare enabling WEP encryption to how WPA encryption is enabled, let's take an example of WPA (this time, we pick 8F37ahr43K as our example pre-shared key). Enabling WPA encryption is a lot like enabling WEP encryption, except you must make one additional decision: You must decide how long an encryption key will be allowed to be used before a new key is assigned. The lower the value, the less time a hacker has to try to "crack" the key. For example, if you set the value to 1800 seconds (which is 30 minutes for you nonmath majors), a key is used for 30 minutes, and then the wireless router and wireless NIC create a new key. If a hacker "cracks" the key within 30 minutes (which is pretty tough to do), the key will only be valuable for the remainder of the 30 minutes before it is switched to an entirely new key, and the hacker would have to start all over.

First, here's an example of setting up WPA on the wireless router:

Step 1 On the Wireless Security subtab again (see Figure 2-20), select **Pre-Shared Key** on the line labeled Security Mode. (On some Linksys products, the selection is called **WPA Pre-Shared Key**.)

Step 2 Select either **TKIP** (for WPA1) or **AES** (for WPA2). If your wireless router and all wireless NICs support AES mode, select it because it is more secure. If any of them do not, select TKIP. You cannot configure some with TKIP and some with AES.

Step 3 On the line labeled WPA Shared Key, enter the pre-shared key you made up (in our example, 8F37ahr43K).

Step 4 On the line labeled Group Key Renewal, enter the number of seconds that you want the key to be used before changing it (see Figure 2-20). We chose 1800 (which is 30 minutes) for this example.

Step 5 Click **Save Settings**.

Figure 2-20   Enabling WPA Encryption on the Wireless Router

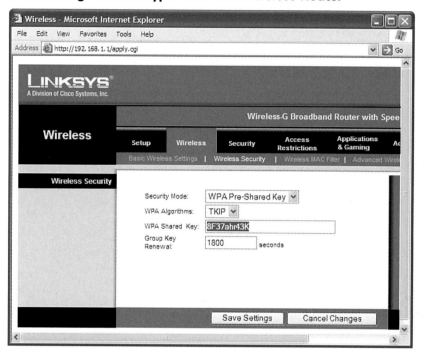

VERY IMPORTANT: **So how long should you set the key renewal period for? There is no great answer, although if you have the value set too low (1 to 2 minutes, for example) it could cause connectivity issues for some NICs. We recommend following manufacturer recommendations (or defaults).**

With WPA, we also then need to tell the super-secret password to each of the devices with wireless cards so that they know how to decode the conversations with the wireless router. Here is an example for a Linksys WPC54GS Wireless-G PCMCIA laptop NIC:

Step 1   Launch the WLAN Monitor Utility, similar to the example earlier where we enabled WEP on a USB-connected wireless NIC.

Step 2   For the Encryption Method, choose **Pre-Shared Key** (see Figure 2-21). (On some Linksys products it is called **WPA Pre-Shared Key**.) Click **Next**.

Step 3   On the line labeled Encryption, select **TKIP** (for WPA1) or **AES** (for WPA2). On the line labeled Passphrase, enter the key phrase you made up (see Figure 2-22). In our example, we chose 8F37ahr43K. Click **Next**.

Figure 2-21   Choose WPA Pre-Shared Key

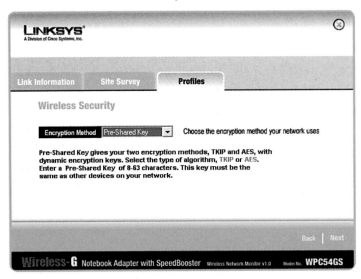

Figure 2-22   Enter the WPA Passphrase

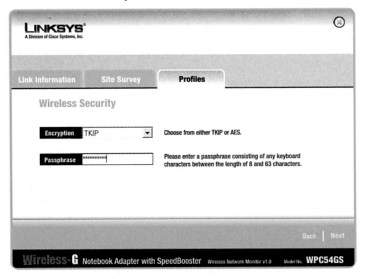

Step 4   In the confirmation window that appears, double-check that Encryption is set to **Pre-Shared Key**, and then click **Save** (see Figure 2-23).

Figure 2-23   Confirm New WPA Settings

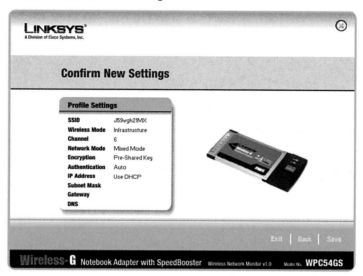

Step 5   Click the **Link Information** tab. If you entered everything correctly, the Signal Strength and Link Quality should reappear as green bars (see Figure 2-24).

If not, you probably entered something incorrectly.

Figure 2-24   You Are Successfully Connected!

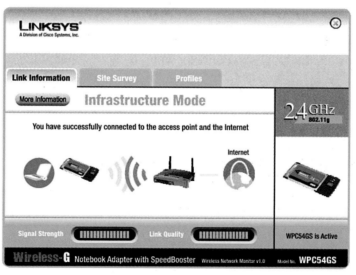

Continue setting up each NIC with the super-secret password, each time checking to see whether the connection is reestablished to the wireless router.

Troubleshooting Tips: Wireless Encryption

If any of the computers do not reestablish communication, items to check include the following:

- Make sure the encryption method chosen on both the wireless router and *all* wireless NICs is the *same*.

- Make sure the passphrase for WEP key generation (or WPA) is entered exactly the *same* on both the wireless router and *all* wireless NICs. The passphrase is case sensitive, which means that *p* is different from *P*. Take care to make sure the entered phrase matches *exactly*, including lowercase and uppercase letters.

- If all else fails, disable encryption on both the wireless router and all wireless network adapters, reverify the connections without encryption turned on, and then start the encryption setup from scratch.

- Read the Troubleshooting and Wireless Security chapters in the installation manuals that came with the Linksys wireless router and Linksys wireless NICs.

Disable Ad-Hoc Networking

As previously mentioned, we recommend for security reasons that you operate your wireless home network in infrastructure mode, meaning a wireless router provides the central point of the network and all wireless computers communicate only with the central point, not to each other directly (which is called ad hoc). This is a relatively low security risk, but there is a small possibility that those sitting next to us in an airport or other public location can try to make an ad-hoc connection directly between their laptop and ours.

Because we only ever plan to use our laptop computers connected to a wireless router in infrastructure mode, we should disable ad-hoc networking mode so that it is not possible for another laptop computer to attempt to make a connection directly to our laptop.

Using the Linksys NIC management utilities (such as WLAN Monitor), we do this by selecting infrastructure mode. When using Windows XP, the operating system manages most wireless NICs for us, and an additional step is required.

If your laptop or NIC does not support doing so, do not worry about it too much; if it is supported, however, why not take advantage of it? Here is how to disable ad-hoc wireless networking in Windows XP for a built-in wireless NIC:

Step 1   Bring up the properties of the wireless NIC.

Click the **Wireless Networks** tab (see Figure 2-25).

In the Preferred Networks section, click the **Advanced** button.

Figure 2-25   Wireless Networks Tab

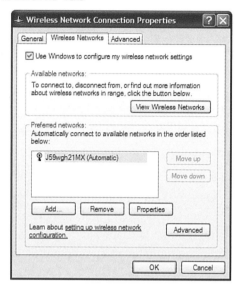

Step 2   Select Access point (infrastructure) networks only (see Figure 2-26).

Figure 2-26   Do Not Allow Ad-Hoc Connections

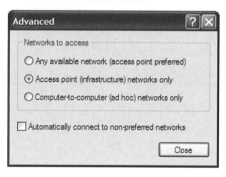

Step 3   Click **Close**.

Step 4   Click **OK** (on the Properties dialog box).

Now, if we encounter another computer with a wireless NIC that attempts to set up an ad-hoc connection, our wireless NIC will not respond to the attempt, keeping our wireless network (and laptop) secure.

Prevent Unintentional Roaming

Wireless networks are a bit like cell phones. Your cell phone tries to find the closest cell tower so that you can get the most bars of signal strength to have high-quality voice calls.

Wireless NICs work in a similar way in that they try to find the wireless router that has the strongest signal. The assumption is that the router it finds is yours because it is the closest and therefore has the strongest signal. However, that is not always true. If you have poor signal strength in a particular room of your house and your neighbor's router actually has a better signal in that room, your wireless NIC might try to roam onto your neighbor's router, unless you instruct it not to.

You do not want your laptop unintentionally hopping over to your neighbor's wireless router whenever it sees a stronger signal or for whatever reason loses connectivity with your own router.

Using the Linksys NIC management utilities (such as WLAN Monitor), this is pretty easy. Simply do not add your neighbor's wireless SSID as a profile.

When using Windows XP to manage wireless connections, an additional step is required:

Step 1   Bring up the properties of the wireless NIC.

Click the **Wireless Networks** tab (see Figure 2-25 earlier).

In the Preferred Networks section, click the **Advanced** button.

Step 2   Make sure **Automatically connect to non-preferred networks** is unchecked (see Figure 2-26 earlier).

Step 3   Click **Close**.

Step 4   Click **OK** (in the Properties dialog box).

Now, if the wireless NIC sees your neighbor's wireless router, it will not try to connect to it because it is not in the list of preferred networks.

Wireless Security Checklist

Wireless networks are extremely beneficial, but you must take some simple steps to protect them. Without taking the steps in this chapter, it is the equivalent of locking the front door and leaving all windows and back doors unlocked and standing open. It is pretty easy (and *so* critical) to add appropriate security. Here's a quick checklist to refer to:

- Change the password on the wireless router from the default (for example, admin).

- Change the SSID from the default (for example, linksys) to a random series of lowercase letters, uppercase letters, and numbers.

- Disable SSID broadcast on the wireless router.

- Enable WEP or WPA encryption on the wireless router and all wireless network adapters. Use the strongest encryption level that all devices support.

- Use a WEP or WPA passphrase that is a random series of lowercase letters, uppercase letters, and numbers.

- Disable ad-hoc wireless networking on all network adapters (applies to Windows XP).

- Disable auto-connection to nonpreferred networks on all wireless network adapters.

Summary

The steps in this chapter are really what most people need to keep their wireless network secure in all but the most extreme cases. The fact is that your SSID can be guessed or discovered, encryption schemes can be cracked (especially WEP), and MAC addresses can be spoofed (via a method called MAC address cloning); but this takes a great deal of skill, time, and money. If you want more protection than this, you can get it, but if you are still worried about wireless security, your best solution might be to stick with a wired network.

One additional wireless security measure that you can take that has not yet been discussed is MAC address locking (often called MAC address filtering). Because each wireless card has a unique identifier called a MAC address, and we know what the MAC addresses are for all of our wireless cards, we could instruct the wireless router to only accept connections from our cards and no one else's. This is called MAC address locking.

Turning on MAC address locking is not trivial and can be a bit of trouble. Remember, with every security measure enabled, you typically lose some flexibility. For example, with MAC address locking enabled, you need to change the configuration on the wireless router if you buy a new wireless card or device. Also, if you have visitors who want temporary Internet access, you would have to grant them access by adding their MAC address to the permission table.

MAC address locking does provide an additional level of protection. If you want to enable it, see Appendix B, "MAC Address Locking for Wireless Security," which is located at http://www.ciscopress.com/1587201364. Click **Appendix** under "More Information."

One final thought for those of you who are really paranoid. There is one way to make your network 100 percent hacker proof: Turn everything off! Going to bed for the night? Leaving town for the weekend? Turn your network off.

If your wireless router and your broadband modem are on the same power strip, you can completely secure you network with the flip of a switch. This will not affect anything at all on your network (unless you are running a server, of course), and it gives you complete peace of mind while you are away from your network.

Finally, do not forget to write down the information, including the SSID, WEP or WPA passphrase, WEP key, and so on. You will need these at some point when adding new devices or computers to your network.

Where to Go for More Information

Here are some good references for more information on security for wireless networks:

http://en.wikipedia.org/wiki/Wired_Equivalent_Privacy

http://en.wikipedia.org/wiki/Wi-Fi_Protected_Access

http://www.wi-fiplanet.com/tutorials/

CHAPTER 3

Tip 3: Use Antivirus Protection

Threat Type: Software based, victim enabled

Examples of Threats:

- Modify, corrupt, or destroy files on your computer

- Corrupt the computer operating system causing unpredictable behavior, poor performance, or security holes

- Unauthorized e-mailing of files or the virus itself to people on your contact list

- Allow a hacker to gain control of your computer through a back door

Our Tips:

- Enable antivirus protection at your *Internet service provider (ISP)* and/or e-mail provider if it is available.

- Install antivirus software on each computer in your home network.

- Set up antivirus software to automatically perform periodic virus scans.

- Make sure any antivirus software automatically retrieves signature updates.

When people talk about computer and network security, they almost always mention computer viruses sooner or later. Even people who do not often use computers have heard about viruses because of all the news hype that surrounds them. In this chapter, we discuss viruses and other malicious code (collectively referred to as *malware*, *bad software*), including where they come from, what they do, how you can protect your computer against them, and how to get rid of them if you do get infected.

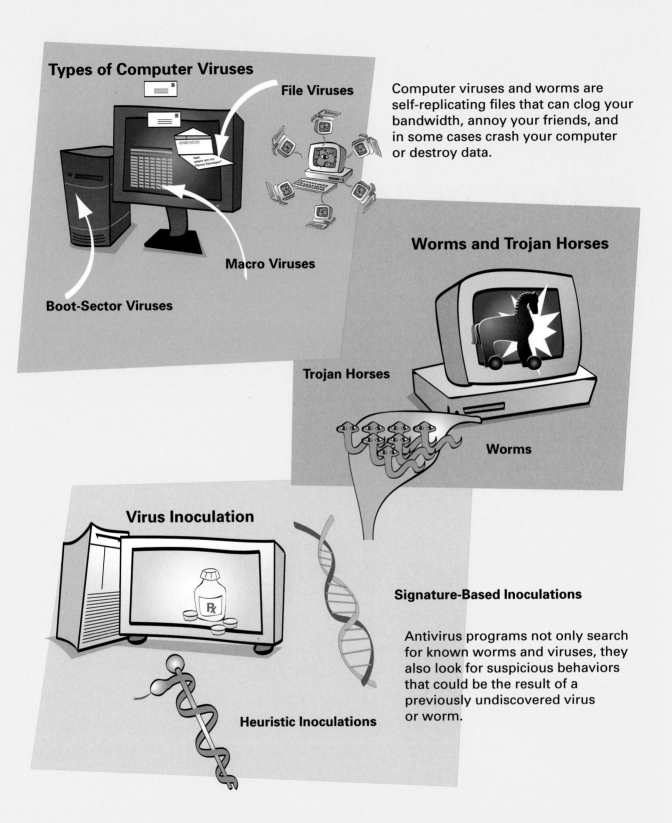

Types of Computer Viruses

File Viruses

Macro Viruses

Boot-Sector Viruses

Computer viruses and worms are self-replicating files that can clog your bandwidth, annoy your friends, and in some cases crash your computer or destroy data.

Worms and Trojan Horses

Trojan Horses

Worms

Virus Inoculation

Signature-Based Inoculations

Antivirus programs not only search for known worms and viruses, they also look for suspicious behaviors that could be the result of a previously undiscovered virus or worm.

Heuristic Inoculations

What Are Computer Viruses?

The term *computer virus* tends to get used for any malicious code created with the intention of harming a computer or slowing network traffic, but a virus is actually a specific type of program. The next few sections give a brief overview of the different kinds of malicious software often lumped into the term *virus*, including a real-world example of each.

VERY IMPORTANT: **You might notice that throughout this book (or any of our books) that we do not name specific viruses, worms, Trojan horses, adware, spyware, and so on. The reason is that one motivation for people who create such programs is the notoriety and publicity that they can create. So, we just choose not to add fuel to that fire.**

Viruses

The definition of a *computer virus* is a program that attaches itself to (or really within) another program (the host) so that it can replicate itself when the host program is run or executed. That's it. You might be surprised that this definition says nothing about removing data, crashing a computer, or any other nasty effects. This is because a virus is defined by its replication behavior, not its effect on the host computer. That said, many viruses do harm data and computers (either intentionally or unintentionally), and any program activity that occurs on your computer or network without your knowledge or consent is a hostile attack against you and your property.

Here is an example. You receive an e-mail like the one in Figure 3-1 from either an unknown person or possibly addressed from someone you do know.

Figure 3-1   Virus E-Mail

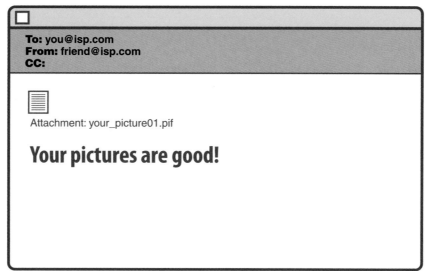

You might think it is okay because it is from a friend or seems harmless because you did share pictures recently, so you double-click the attachment, installing a virus on your computer. The virus then searches through your Microsoft Outlook Express address book and e-mails a copy of itself to all your friends and family.

Some viruses are designed to remove or replace data or corrupt computer systems. These types of viruses tend to be an exception, because they are extremely difficult to create. Just as worrisome are the viruses created by people who are not skilled programmers, because their programs tend to be unpredictable. In the off chance that a virus created by an unskilled programmer does replicate in the "wild" (on the Internet), there is really no telling what the program will do.

Worms

Worms are similar to viruses in that their defining characteristic is self replication. Unlike viruses, however, a worm's primary function is *not* to do damage to a computer, but just to keep replicating, and replicating, and replicating.

Worms also differ from viruses in that they do not require an executable file. Worms exploit security holes in computer systems or software programs. You might be thinking that simple replication without harming or removing files is not so bad, but replication can be so explosive that your computer performance slows to a crawl, your broadband connection gets clogged, and if enough computers become infected, the entire Internet can experience problems.

Figure 3-2 shows an example of how a worm attack and replication occurs. It starts by a hacker (or whomever) creating a new type of worm and launching it to infect others and start the replication.

Figure 3-2   Virus/Worm Infection Example

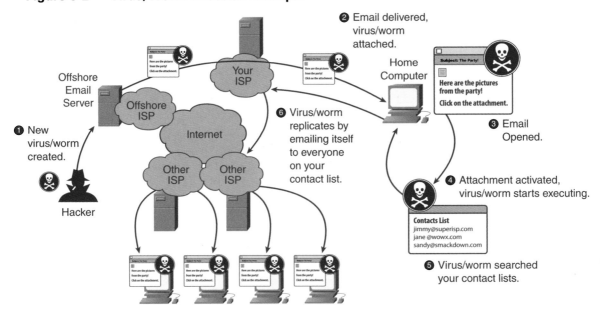

The worm may show up at your computer in any number of ways, most commonly via e-mail or downloading "free" software from the Internet. In this example, the worm (a virus would behave in a similar way) shows up in the form of an e-mail pretending to be pictures from a recent party. The user unknowingly double-clicks the e-mail attachment, and the worm starts executing.

When triggered, it searches your computer for e-mail addresses of your friends and family (and business associates) by dipping into your e-mail program's contacts list. The worm then e-mails itself to everyone in your list, and the replication continues.

Another type of worm requires no action by a human to spread. It simply exploits a weakness or bug in the operating system software and spreads like wildfire directly from PC to PC. Imagine this process starting out on a few hundred computers, each e-mailing 20 or 100 others, and soon enough hundreds of thousands of computers across the globe are infected. One of the most well-known worms infected more than 350,000 computers within 13 hours of release. At the peak of the spread, more than 2000 new computers were being infected every minute.

Whereas computer virus outbreaks used to be measured in days, worm outbreaks are now measured in minutes or seconds because of the speed of the Internet and ubiquitous availability of e-mail.

It is worth noting that many people (including those in the media) lump all these types of files into the virus category when many are in fact worms.

Trojan Horses

Trojan horses are probably the most unknown type of malicious program but are potentially the most devastating to those who get infected by them. Similar to viruses and worms, Trojan horses typically arrive at your computer in an e-mail attachment or as a hidden gift within a "free" software program you downloaded. Just like the horse from Homer's epic, a nasty surprise is waiting inside this gift. *Trojan horses* are programs that give a hacker access to your computer. After the "gift" file is opened, the hacker's program is also opened and that's when the trouble starts. Some of the more common programs are keystroke loggers and remote control programs:

- **Key stroke loggers** collect everything you type on your keyboard (including passwords, usernames, and credit card numbers). After a certain amount of data is collected, the information is sent to the hacker (without your knowledge, of course).

- **Remote-control programs** enable hackers to take over your machine, allowing them to go through your files and data or use your machine to attack another computer.

Figure 3-3 shows an example of how a Trojan horse attack occurs. It starts by a hacker (or whomever) creating a new type of Trojan horse and launching it to infect others.

Figure 3-3   Trojan Horse Infection Example

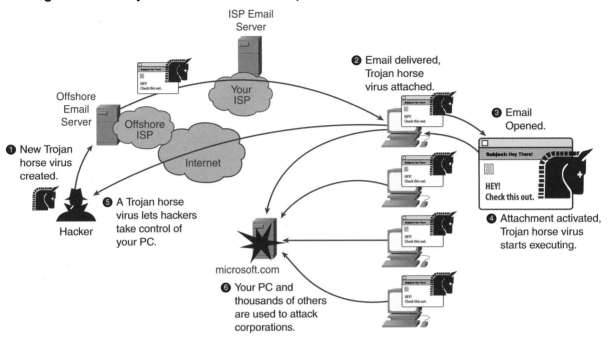

When triggered, the Trojan horse deposits a program onto your computer and reports back to the author, handing over the keys to access your computer.

They might now use your computer as an anonymous launching point to conduct illegal activity, such as hacking others or enlisting thousands of computers to attack a corporate website. (See the discussion about bot armies in Chapter 1, "Tip 1: Use Firewalls.")

Imagine your embarrassment when the FBI knocks on our door to tell you your computer was used in an attempt to shut down a corporate or government network.

Commonsense Approach to Computer Viruses

It is actually pretty hard to keep yourself from being infected with a virus. It is a bit like visiting a doctor's office or preschool: You can watch what you touch, who you sit near, and wash your hands, but you can still end up with a cold.

The first line of defense against computer viruses, worms, and Trojan horses is common sense. You can do some fairly simple things to prevent infection:

- Do not open any e-mail (especially attachments) from people whom you do not know.

- Many recent viruses replicate by sending themselves to people in your contact list, so it is possible to receive a virus e-mail from someone you know, even without that person knowing he or she sent it.

- Preview any e-mail thoroughly before opening attachments. If you have any suspicion whatsoever, call the sender on the phone and ask whether he or she sent the e-mail.

- Avoid "free" software, offers, and opportunities. Ask yourself why they are giving valuable stuff away.

- If you use an e-mail program, such as Outlook, that gives you the option of viewing e-mails in plain text or HTML, set the default to plain text. Some viruses now take advantage of HTML and auto-launch as soon as the e-mail is opened. If you only view in plain text, any attached virus must be manually opened (which means at least you have a fighting chance).

- There is also a preview pane in Outlook that does actually open the e-mail and can launch a worm or virus. You can turn the feature off for some added protection.

VERY IMPORTANT: **If you have children who use the Internet from a computer at home, set a rule that all downloads should be approved by Mom or Dad. This is good advice for malicious software and for some topics discussed later in the book.**

Unfortunately, common sense does not save you from every infection, and anyone who has been using the Internet any period of time has likely been hit with a virus or worm. We have been hit. Everyone we know has been hit, and so has pretty much every company on the Fortune 1000. So, obviously, common sense is not enough. Fortunately, we have antivirus programs that are both cheap and effective.

How Antivirus Works

Antivirus programs work by searching computer data for viruses and malicious software code (which includes viruses, worms, and Trojan horses) and then removing the infections they find. Several elements of any antivirus software are important to understand:

- **Scanning engine**—The software that runs on your computer and searches for viruses in the computer's memory and files on the hard disk.

- **Active scanning**—Scanning for viruses after an infection has gotten there is only half the battle; active scanning searches arriving e-mail, downloaded software, and other data newly arriving into your computer.

- **Signatures**—Each virus has a unique signature, kind of like fingerprints, that identifies it and gives itself away to the antivirus program.

- **Auto-update**—New viruses are created every day, so the antivirus software must be frequently updated with new signatures.

- **Heuristics**—Sometimes viruses can be detected even before a signature is identified.

These concepts are discussed in more detail in the rest of this chapter.

Virus Detection

Just about every antivirus program on the market today works by recognizing the so-called *signature* inherent in all viruses. In this case, a signature refers to the unique sets of bit arrangements within the virus code. Antivirus software programs contain thousands of signatures. Figure 3-4 shows how the virus-detection process works. As new e-mail and data arrive at a computer, the antivirus software checks the new information against its list of known virus signatures.

Figure 3-4   Virus Detection Using Known Virus Signatures

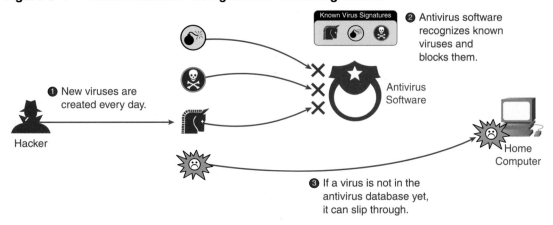

These programs run in the background and do not generally affect the performance of your computer unless you have very processor-intensive programs running (such as high-end games or a *computer-assisted design* [CAD] program).

When a match is found, an additional detailed comparison is made against the actual virus program to protect against false positives. If that comparison is positive, the e-mail or download is blocked, and the data is flagged for removal from your computer.

When a new virus is discovered, teams of engineers at the antivirus software companies begin working to identify the unique signature. After the signature is identified and distributed to everyone who purchased the antivirus software program, the program adds the signature to the list of what it looks for during the scanning process.

During the interim period between a new virus release and the discovery and distribution of the new signature for that virus, antivirus programs do not have the signature necessary to detect the virus. How to block these "time-zero" viruses is the focus of much work right now.

Virus Prevention

One of the biggest problems today is that an Internet virus or worm can travel around the Internet faster than news about the virus or worm. So, even if the antivirus people start working on finding the signature as soon as the virus launches, by the time they find and distribute the signature, the virus could have gone around the world. In most cases, this is exactly what happens. Therefore, the antivirus people are under pressure to protect their customers from being affected by worms and viruses before a "cure" is found. Their answer to this is heuristic detection.

Heuristic detection looks at behavior patterns of files and executables on your machine. If a program launches and starts behaving oddly or in a virus/wormlike way, the program is flagged, and the user is notified. Figure 3-5 shows an example. Suppose the virus that escaped detection in Figure 3-4 earlier now starts executing. It searches the Outlook Express address book on your computer and attempts to start mass e-mailing itself to everyone on your contact list.

Figure 3-5   Virus Prevention Using Heuristics

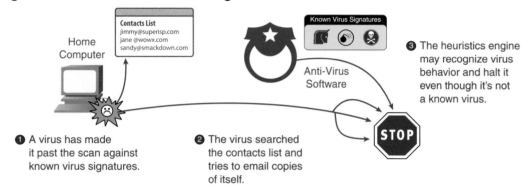

It is possible that if heuristic detection is enabled, the antivirus program might recognize the behavior of the program as viruslike, and halt or quarantine it until further notice.

Unlike signature-based detection, heuristic detection will also notice and flag remote-control behavior and keystroke loggers, offering protection against the most common Trojan horse attacks. Although heuristic detection greatly improves your time-zero (the early moments of a virus or worm explosion) defense, there are some limitations:

- There is an occurrence of false positives (flagging events that are not virus or worm related). This can get annoying for some folks, who then might just turn the feature off.

- Some virus programmers out there can spoof or fake out the behavior software and get around the defense that the antivirus programs provide.

Even with these limitations, however, behavior-based protection software is worth enabling and recommended. Heuristics are included in most of the major antivirus software programs, including those from McAfee, Symantec, Trend Micro, and Zone Labs.

Inoculating Yourself Against Computer Viruses

You have an increasing number of options for where you can install antivirus software to protect your home network. Figure 3-6 shows the possible locations. First, antivirus software *must* be installed on each computer in your home network.

Figure 3-6   Where You Need to Have Antivirus Protection

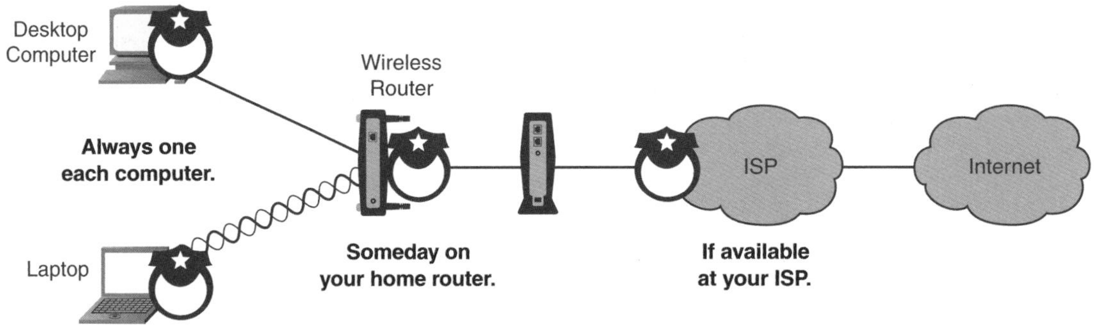

In addition, many ISPs offer a feature to turn on antivirus protection for your e-mail account in their network. If this is an option with your ISP, definitely turn it on. It is much better to intercept and destroy viruses at your ISP than to let them reach your home network and then try to detect and destroy them.

Finally, antivirus software is working its way into home network routers. When widely available, this would be a great place to enforce your antivirus security.

So, you may be asking yourself, "If I turn antivirus on at my ISP, do I need to have it on my computers, too?" The answer is yes, absolutely. Antivirus at your ISP typically only protects e-mail and does little to protect the other communication paths between your computers and the Internet. Only computer-based antivirus can catch everything into and out of your PC today.

What about antivirus on your home network router? Well, it's possible that because the router sees all the traffic into and out of your computers that it might become the preferred enforcement point for antivirus, and you would not need it on each computer. This is probably where antivirus is going, but it is not quite there today. In the meantime, we recommend buying a software program that specifically provides antivirus protection for each of your computers.

Turning On Antivirus at Your ISP

Many ISPs offer built-in antivirus protection within their e-mail services. Check with your service provider to see whether this is an option. If it is, it is certainly something you should take advantage of. Many, many viruses multiply themselves by using e-mail to grow the infection to other computers. Detecting and stopping these viruses inside the e-mail system of the service provider is preferable to waiting until they are already inside your home network.

How to enable antivirus protection with your service provider will vary widely and depend entirely on how they have chosen to set up their services. Enabling the protection is easy. We use EarthLink as an example:

Step 1   Log in to the EarthLink My Account page using your account user ID and password.

Step 2   Click **TURN ON Virus Blocker** (see Figure 3-7).

Figure 3-7   Enabling the EarthLink Virus Blocker

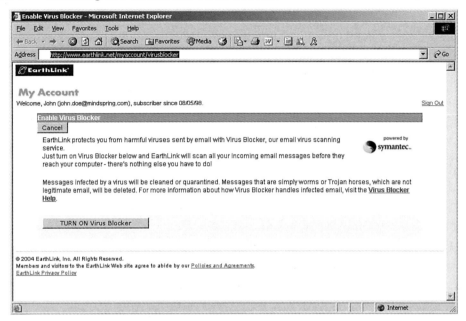

When new e-mail arrives to your mailbox at EarthLink, it is scanned for viruses. If it is found to be infected, the e-mail is routed to a special quarantine folder so that it will never be downloaded to your computer's e-mail inbox file.

Installing Antivirus Software on Your Computers

As discussed in Chapter 1, you have a couple of options for purchasing antivirus software programs for each of your home computers. You can purchase only antivirus or pay a little more money for an entire security bundle. Security bundles are offered by the major security software vendors, and include a whole suite of protection, including antivirus, firewall, spyware/adware blocking, parental control, antispam, and so on.

We recommend checking out the security bundles from the leading security software vendors in Table 3-1.

Table 3-1   Leading Security Software Bundle Vendors

Security Bundle Provider	Internet Address
McAfee Internet Security Suite	http://www.mcafee.com
Symantec Norton Internet Security 200x	http://www.symantec.com
Trend Micro PC-cillin Internet Security	http://www.trendmicro.com
ZoneAlarm Security Suite	http://www.zonelabs.com

Whether you decide to opt for the bundle or just for the antivirus software, the steps and descriptions here are roughly the same.

Figure 3-8 shows the main control panel for McAfee's product (the example shown is part of the security bundle).

Figure 3-8   McAfee VirusScan (Component of McAfee Internet Security Suite)

Figure 3-9 shows the main control panel for Symantec's product (the example shown is also part of the security bundle).

Figure 3-9   Symantec's Norton AntiVirus (Component of Norton Internet Security 200x)

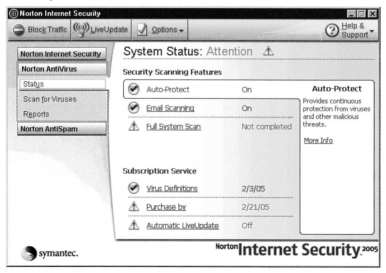

All four (McAfee, Symantec, Trend Micro, and Zone Labs) are good products. All also require an annual subscription fee to receive virus signature updates (*which is critical*). Shop around and compare. Many have free 30-day trials you can download so that you can find which one is right for you.

Scanning Your Computer for Viruses

When you install antivirus software, it will perform an initial scan of your computer to detect whether existing infections exist. After that, the software typically is set up to perform periodic scans to ensure that no infections find their way onto your computer.

Figure 3-10 shows an example of the McAfee product performing a scan.

Figure 3-10 Scanning for Viruses with McAfee VirusScan

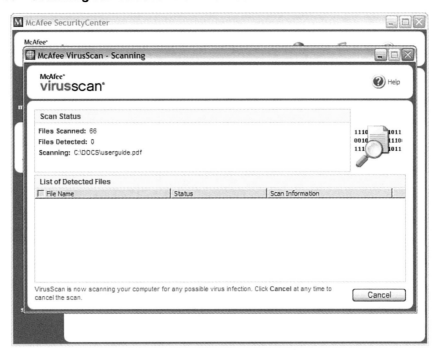

In this case, as shown in Figure 3-11, nine infected files were found on the computer, including two known viruses and seven undesirable adware programs (see Chapter 5, "Tip 5: Lock Out Spyware and Adware"). The antivirus scanner recommends what to do with the infected files (fix, delete, or quarantine them).

Figure 3-12 shows a scan with the Symantec antivirus product on another computer. In this case, five infected files were found and deleted.

Figure 3-11   McAfee Scan Completed and Viruses Deleted

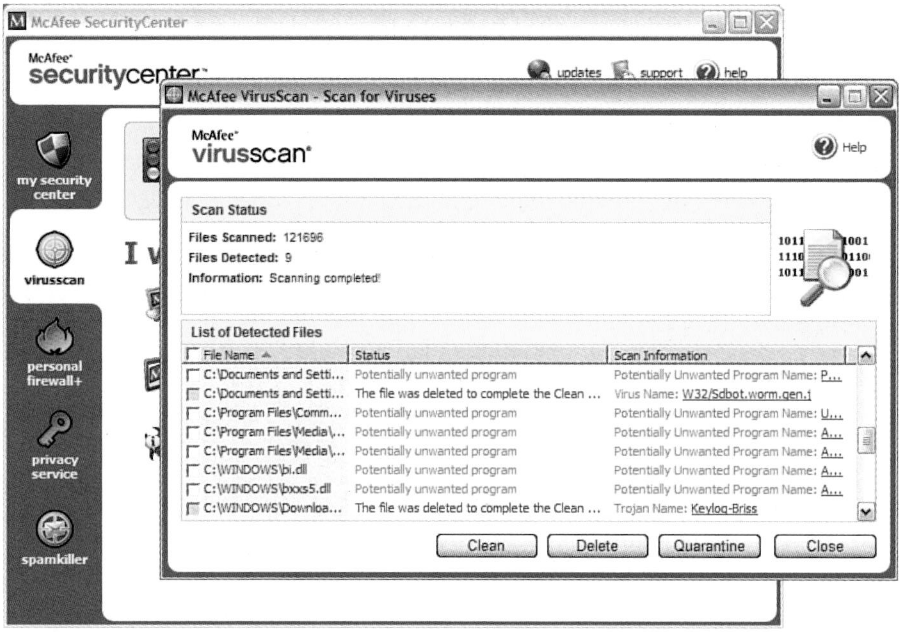

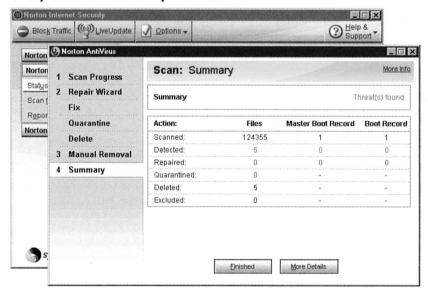

Figure 3-12   Symantec Scan Completed and Viruses Deleted

Most infections can be automatically repaired by the antivirus software. Severe infections may require more work. In general, clicking the **Fix** (for Norton) or **Clean** (for McAfee) buttons tells the antivirus software to attempt to repair the file to its original state; clicking **Delete** tells the software to trash the file; and clicking **Quarantine** tells the software to isolate the file from the rest of your files by placing it in a special holding area.

When it doubt, click **Fix** or **Clean** (or the equivalent in the antivirus software you are using). If that fails, then click **Delete**.

Blocking New Virus Infections

Scanning the computer memory and files on the hard disk is a necessary periodic procedure. However, only doing disk scans is a little like waiting for the bandits to sell the stolen jewelry before apprehending them. Wouldn't it be better to catch them as they first try to break into the store?

All the antivirus programs have a feature for active scans, meaning whenever you receive a new e-mail, browse a web page, download a new file, or edit an existing file, the antivirus scanner kicks in to make sure no virus is introduced.

Active scanning is usually enabled by default with antivirus programs. Figure 3-13 shows an example of enabling this protection (assuming it was not set as the default).

Figure 3-13   Enabling Active Scanning with McAfee VirusScan

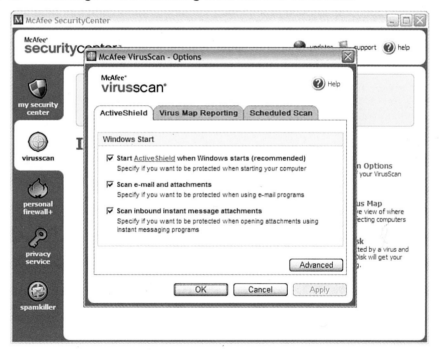

In general, you want to make sure that the antivirus program starts up its active scanner when Windows boots and that e-mail and attachments are scanned automatically, both incoming and outgoing.

Enabling Unknown Virus Detection (Heuristics)

As discussed earlier, we also want to turn on the ability to try to detect unknown viruses from their general behavior rather than from only specific signatures. For the McAfee product, this is done by configuring the scan options. Figure 3-14 shows the dialog window.

Figure 3-14   Turning On Unknown Virus Detection with McAfee VirusScan

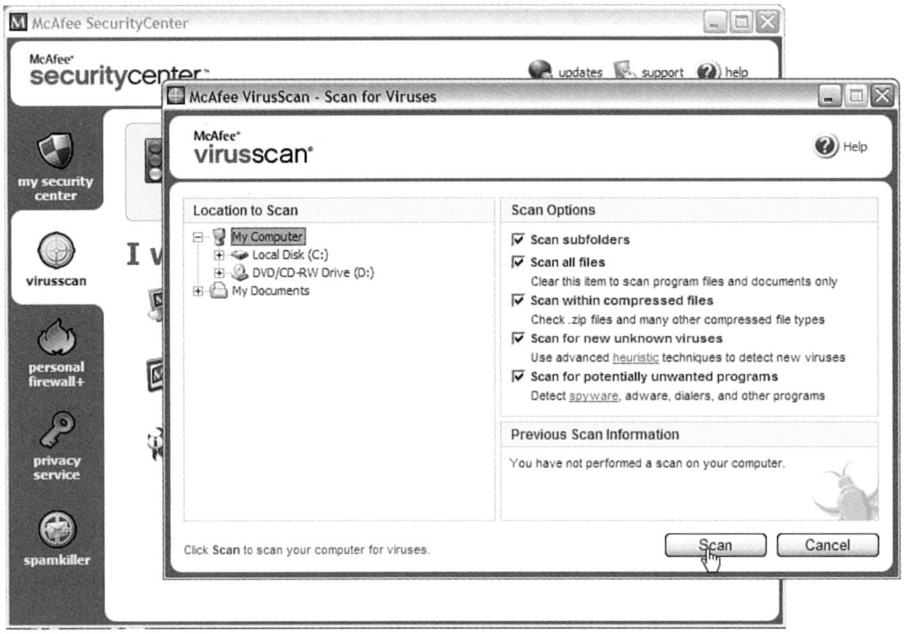

Make sure that the **Scan for new unknown viruses** option is checked.

The Symantec option has a similar feature, called Bloodhound (see Figure 3-15).

Figure 3-15   Turning On Unknown Virus Detection with Symantec Norton AntiVirus

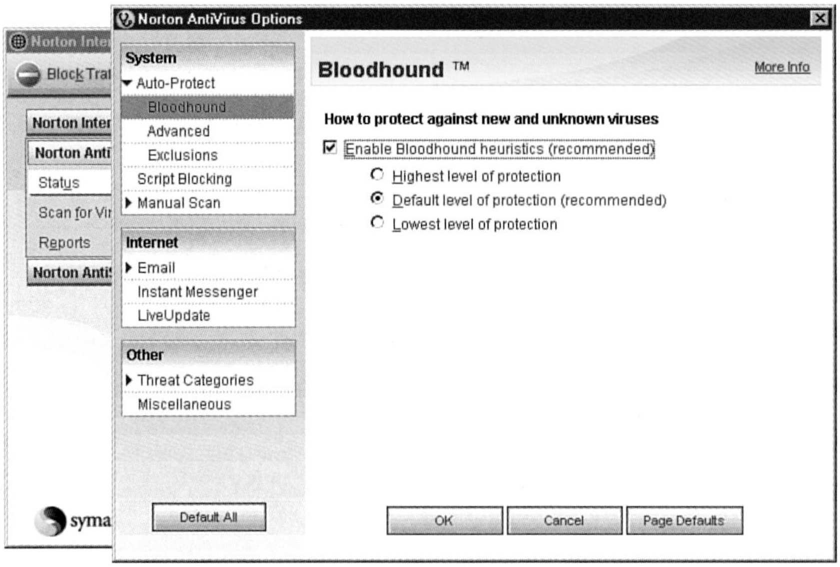

Make sure that the **Enable Bloodhound heuristics** option is checked.

Keep in mind that occasionally with this function, you will get some false positives, meaning the antivirus software will think a normal operating program is performing a suspicious action and raise the flag to you.

An example is whenever you choose to install a legitimate software program. It might trigger the antivirus software to raise a warning and prompt you for confirmation that you asked for the software to be installed.

Updating Your Virus Signatures

Another critical task to do with any antivirus program is to make sure it receives updated virus signatures automatically. It is usually the default, but Figure 3-16 shows how to enable automatic updates for the Symantec product.

Figure 3-16   Turning On Automatic Updates with Symantec Antivirus

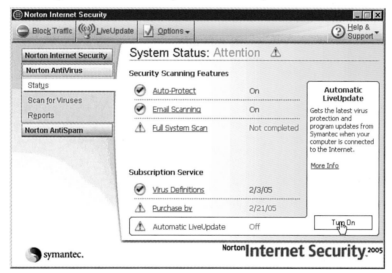

Figure 3-17 shows the result after an update of the virus signatures has run.

Automatic updates require an active subscription with the antivirus software vendor. We cannot express how important it is to maintain the most current level of virus signatures (this means check your program for regular updates). If your signatures are even three to six months out of date, you are highly likely to be infected by one of the dozens of new viruses and worms that are created every month.

If you turn your computer (or even your network router) off when you are not using it, you will probably need to manually check for updates even if you have the auto-update feature enabled.

You might reason that you can cancel your subscription and get away with an older set of signatures and then rely on the heuristic scanning. Several evaluations have shown heuristics to be only approximately 60 percent to 70 percent effective in detecting unknown viruses. Some heuristic scanners also rely on the latest set of signatures to be most effective at detecting virus behaviors. The point is, you cannot rely on heuristics to fill the gap for not keeping your signatures current.

Figure 3-17   Signatures Are Updated

Windows Live OneCare

Windows is slowly integrating security functions. In Chapter 1, you saw that Windows XP offers a built-in firewall function. In Chapter 5, you will see a similar Windows built-in spyware/adware function called Windows Defender. For antivirus, Windows does not yet offer an integrated product, but there is a service named Windows Live OneCare that looks promising for integrated antivirus protection.

The intended pricing for this service looks comparable to other antivirus subscriptions. If you are interested, you can obtain the software beta (or production when it is released), at this link:

http://www.windowsonecare.com

After you install the OneCare software, the main control panel looks as shown in Figure 3-18.

Figure 3-18   Windows Live OneCare Main Status Panel

In addition to antivirus, the OneCare panel has integration with the functions for firewall, computer tune-up, file backup, and operating system updates.

By clicking **View or change settings** on the main OneCare panel, it is possible to change the antivirus settings, as shown in Figure 3-19.

Figure 3-19   OneCare Antivirus Settings

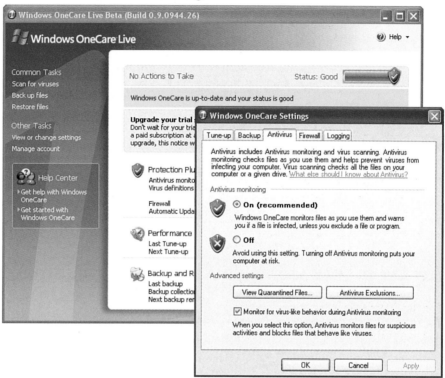

Check the **Monitor for virus-like behavior** box to enable heuristic scanning (covered previously in this chapter).

Figure 3-20 shows the result of a virus scan. This time the computer was free of worms and viruses.

OneCare's antivirus program has many of the same features and operations as the other antivirus programs, including heuristic scanning, automatic updates, and active scanning of e-mail and file accesses.

It is not clear whether OneCare supports the same extensive list of known virus signatures as the other packages. A look at the OneCare threat list shows only a list of viruses identified as Top Threats. More information will undoubtedly be available when the product is officially released in mid-2006.

Figure 3-20   OneCare Scan Completed

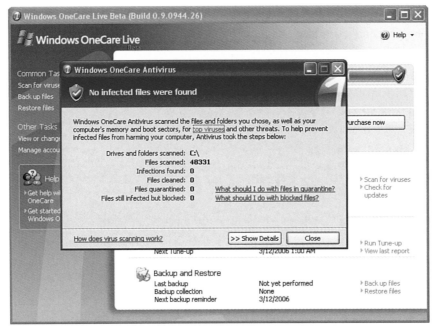

What to Do If You Think You've Been Infected

Having antivirus software installed and operating (including at least weekly signature updates) should keep you free of viruses the vast majority of the time. However, occasionally you might be one of the first to come across a new virus and can still become infected.

Chapter 1 contains some tips for recognizing malicious processes and blocking their access to the Internet.

In addition, you might be able to detect the virus with an online scanning tool. Both McAfee and Symantec offer an online security scan. The websites are here:

> http://us.mcafee.com/root/mfs/default.asp?cid=9913

> http://security.symantec.com

Figure 3-21 shows the Symantec online scan main dialog.

If either the online scan or normal antivirus scanning detects a virus and does not automatically remove it, there is information on all the major antivirus vendors' websites about how to remedy severe infections.

Some infections may be so severe that irreversible damage is done to the operating system. This severity might require reloading the operating system from scratch. If you encounter a severe infection that the antivirus software cannot automatically repair, and you are not comfortable repairing it yourself, get help from someone who knows what he is doing.

Figure 3-21   Using Symantec Online Security Scan

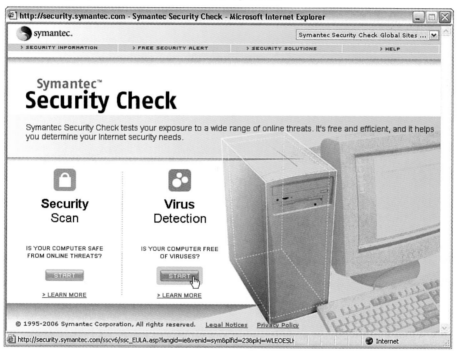

Symantec offers virus-removal tools here:

> http://symantec.com/avcenter/home_homeoffice/tools.list.html

Figure 3-22 shows the directory of the Symantec virus-removal tools. To use one, match the virus name identified by the online or antivirus scan to the removal tool. Then download and run it on your computer.

Figure 3-22   Virus-Removal Tools

If at all possible, back up your files prior to running any virus-removal tools, in case the removal process causes the computer operating system to become unstable.

Summary

No guarantee certifies that having antivirus software will stop all viruses from reaching your computer. One thing that is guaranteed is that if you do not use antivirus software, you will become infected by a virus, worm, Trojan horse, or other form of malware at some point. It is not if, but a matter of when.

Antivirus is also not the only precaution that is necessary to combat viruses. Firewalls (see Chapter 1), operating system updates (see Chapter 4, "Tip 4: Keep Your Software Updated"), and common sense (see Chapter 10, "Tip 10: Use Common Sense") are also integral parts of the strategy you need to implement to minimize the chance of a virus infection and subsequent effects.

Where to Go for More Information

You can find additional information on viruses, worms, and Trojan horses from the following websites:

http://symantec.com/avcenter/home_homeoffice/

http://www.microsoft.com/athome/security/viruses/

http://vil.nai.com/vil/

CHAPTER 4

Tip 4: Keep Your Software Updated

Threat Type: Software based

Examples of Threats:

- Exploiting a security flaw in the operating system (for example, Windows) to perform an unauthorized action, such as gaining control of the computer or installing a malicious program

- Exploiting a weakness in the operating system to steal private information such as passwords

- Exploiting a security flaw in any program installed on your computer, similar to exploiting operating system flaws or weaknesses

Our Tips:

- Enable Windows Automatic Updates (or the equivalent for your operating system) with a weekly update frequency.

- If automatic updates are not supported by your operating system, set yourself a reminder on your PC to do it manually.

- Create restore points periodically and after each time you install new software.

- Regularly update programs installed on your computer with updates from the vendor, especially any program that accesses the Internet, such as browsers, e-mail handlers, media players, and instant messaging.

- Use antivirus software (see Chapter 3, "Tip 3: Use Antivirus Protection").

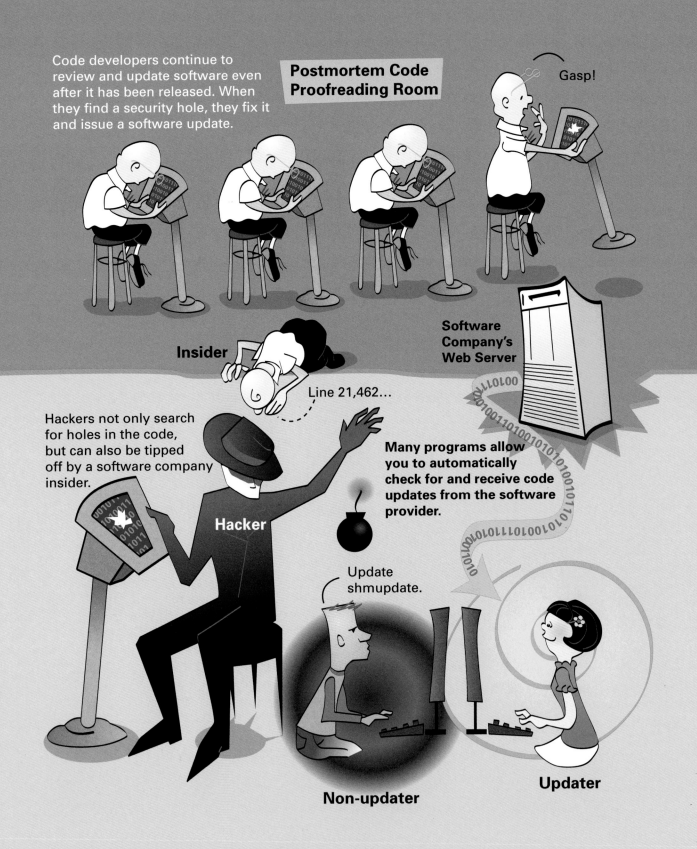

Code developers continue to review and update software even after it has been released. When they find a security hole, they fix it and issue a software update.

Postmortem Code Proofreading Room

Gasp!

Insider

Line 21,462...

Software Company's Web Server

Hackers not only search for holes in the code, but can also be tipped off by a software company insider.

Many programs allow you to automatically check for and receive code updates from the software provider.

Hacker

Update shmupdate.

Non-updater

Updater

One of the key potential security holes in your home network is outdated software. This includes the Windows operating system itself, programs that you have installed, and even security software programs such as antivirus and personal software firewalls.

Computer software is an intricate collection of programs, files, and features that all must work and talk together to have a functioning home computer. There are literally tens of millions of lines of computer instructions (called code), and it is nearly impossible to get them all correct the first time when a new operating system such as Windows XP or Windows Vista is released.

Sometimes mistakes or oversights are made when the programmers write the software that make it possible for people to "punch a hole" in a piece of software and sometimes exploit such a hole to run malicious software code, such as a virus.

Why Software Needs to Be Updated

Over time, the holes in software are found, via additional testing by the companies that created the software or by hackers or others who use the holes for malicious purposes. As soon as holes are discovered, the software company updates their software to close them. It is a little bit like having a pet mouse that keeps figuring a way out of his cage. You can close one escape route, and the little crafty devil finds another, so you close that one, and so on.

For example, recently a vulnerability was found in Windows Media Player 10 that allows hackers to supply Media Player a bitmap file (.BMP) that specifies a size of zero but contains data. When Media Player tries to read the file, it causes a failure in the program and allows hackers to potentially execute some malicious code. A computer virus could be written exploiting such a hole and then those lured to a website with the picture (bitmap file) could trigger the virus on their computer.

The *United States Computer Emergency Readiness Team* (US-CERT) collects and publishes a database of such vulnerabilities so that computer operating system vendors such as Microsoft and security software vendors such as Symantec can incorporate corrections and detection mechanisms into their software. You can find the complete threat list here:

http://www.kb.cert.org/vuls/

Instead of reading such a list daily and worrying about it, the best course of action is to keep your software current. Regularly updating your software plugs such holes so that viruses and other malicious programs can no longer exploit them to do bad things inside your computer.

Updating Your Operating System

The most targeted software programs are the most commonly used, including Microsoft Windows, Microsoft Outlook, and Microsoft Internet Explorer. So just as important as installing a firewall program or antivirus program is making sure that the Windows operating system itself and its various software components are the latest versions. The folks at Microsoft continually release updates to improve functionality, but also to patch security holes that are found; so, having the latest and greatest software is yet another critical security measure for your home network.

You can update all Windows products over your broadband Internet connection, which makes it easy to stay current.

For any of you still on dialup (or needing a critical update when broadband is not available), you can still download updates, but it could end up taking quite a long time. Think about the time of day that works best with your usage patterns and download speed.

Enabling Automatic Updates

In most cases, you should set up Windows to automatically update itself, because you will not likely remember to do so yourself often enough. How automatic your update occurs depends on the version of Windows you are running.

If you are running Windows XP, it has a built-in feature for fetching and installing the latest updates to itself from the Microsoft website. For Windows XP Service Pack 2 (SP2), the steps are easy:

> **Step 1**   Click **Start > Control Panel > Security Center** to launch it (see Figure 4-1). Click **Automatic Updates**.

Figure 4-1   Windows XP Security Center

> **Step 2**   Select **Automatic (recommended)** and set how often you want to update (see Figure 4-2). The longest should be about a week.

Figure 4-2   Turning On Automatic Updates to Windows XP

Now whenever your computer is running and connected to the Internet, it will poll the Microsoft website at the time you set for the latest and greatest software components and compare them with the versions you have installed on your computer. If a new security update is needed, it is installed automatically on your computer. Some updates might require the computer to be restarted before they can be activated on your computer.

If you would rather decide when to actually install the updates, you can select **Download updates for me, but let me choose when to install them**. When updates download, you are prompted that "Windows updates are ready to install," and you can approve the installation.

For older versions of Windows, automatic updates may or may not be possible. For Windows 2000, you can install a similar Automatic Updates feature from here:

>   http://support.microsoft.com/kb/327850/EN-US/

For Windows 98, the Automatic Updates feature is not available, but Microsoft does offer a Critical Update Notification utility, available from here:

>   http://support.microsoft.com/kb/224420/EN-US/

This utility notifies you anytime there is an important update to the operating system. You must then go to the Microsoft update website and manually trigger the update (see the next section).

Finally, if you are using Windows ME, you can update your operating system by following this link:

>   http://support.microsoft.com/kb/268331/

Manual Operating System Updates

If your version of Windows does not provide for automatic updates, or you just want to do them manually, you can do so via the Microsoft update website directly:

http://windowsupdate.microsoft.com/

The steps to do so are as follows:

VERY IMPORTANT: **Windows Update is being replaced by Microsoft Update. If you see this phrase, it does the same thing as Windows Update.**

Step 1 Launch your web browser (such as Internet Explorer) and go to http://windowsupdate.microsoft.com (see Figure 4-3).

Figure 4-3   Windows Update Site

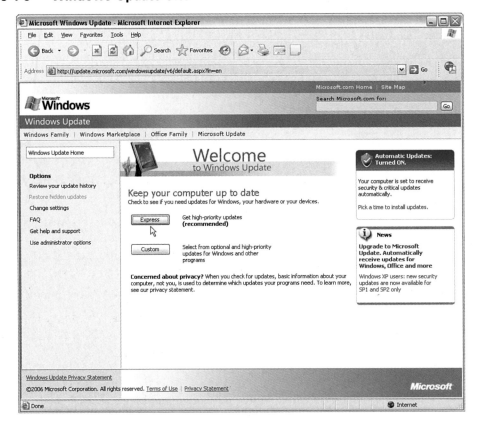

Step 2 Depending on the Windows version, you might follow a different path to updates. If you see a **Scan for Updates** button, click to determine which updates are needed on your computer. After scanning is complete, click the **Review and Install Updates** button and

follow the instructions. The updates are installed over the Internet to your computer (see Figure 4-4).

Another possibility is you will see two buttons: Express and Custom. Clicking **Express** installs the high-priority updates such as known security issues. You are not prompted to choose which to install. Clicking **Custom** presents a list of high-priority and optional updates and allows you to select which to install. In general, Express is the option you want to choose.

Figure 4-4   Windows Update in Progress

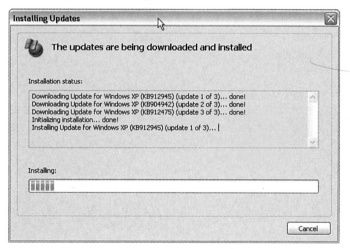

Typically, you must reboot your computer after you have installed updates (especially if security updates are included).

Updating Your Software Programs

Windows Automatic Updates takes care of the Windows operating system and any major components, including Outlook Express, Internet Explorer, and Microsoft Office.

However, it is also important to update other software programs on your computer that are non-Microsoft, such as media players (for example, RealPlayer or QuickTime), e-mail programs, instant messaging, and communications programs (AOL IM or Skype, for instance), and so on.

VERY IMPORTANT: **Often when you install a new software program, you are asked to supply an e-mail address to register the software to receive information on updates and new versions. It is a good idea to register your major software programs so that you do get notified by the vendor upon release of important updates.**

Sometimes, hackers exploit holes in these types of programs, just like they do the Windows operating system, so it is important to keep them current, too. Some have automatic update notifications reminding you when you need to update.

Figures 4-5 and 4-6 show an update example for RealPlayer. To determine whether an update is available, open RealPlayer and select **Help > About**. Then, click the **Check for Update** button, as shown in Figure 4-5.

Figure 4-5   Checking for Updates with RealPlayer

When the software checks itself against the latest available, it determines that several possible updates are available, including one related to security (see Figure 4-6).

Figure 4-6   Selecting a Security Update for Download

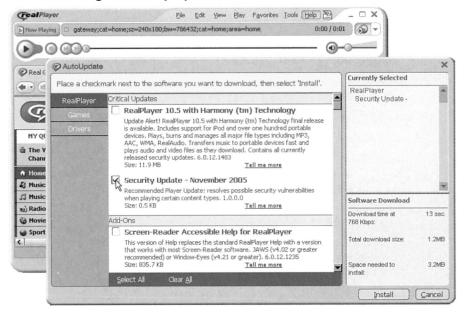

Clicking **Install** will then cause the update to occur.

Each software program is slightly different, and we cannot cover all of them. But, they will usually follow a process similar to this example. Some programs automatically check for updates; others might require a manual step.

Using Windows Restore Points

Windows *restore points* are a relatively new concept starting with Windows XP that enable you to restore the operating system and computer software environment to a previous point in time.

View restore points like the Undo function in Microsoft Word or like a save point in a video game. If you make a mistake (or in the case of a video game, get killed), you can just go back and pick up where you left off without having to start over from the beginning (meaning reloading your computer from scratch).

Restore points are similar. Each time after you install software or otherwise make significant changes to the computer's configuration, a snapshot is taken of the configuration.

Restore points are useful in a number of ways, including if you inadvertently install some software that causes the computer system to become unstable, get infected by a virus, or otherwise mess up your computer, even to the point of no longer booting.

Figure 4-7 shows an example of how Windows XP restore points work. Suppose that we purchased a computer in a fairly pristine state with just the Windows XP operating system on it. An initial restore point has been created with a date of March 1 (typically by the installation process itself).

Figure 4-7   How Windows XP Restore Points Work

System Restore Database

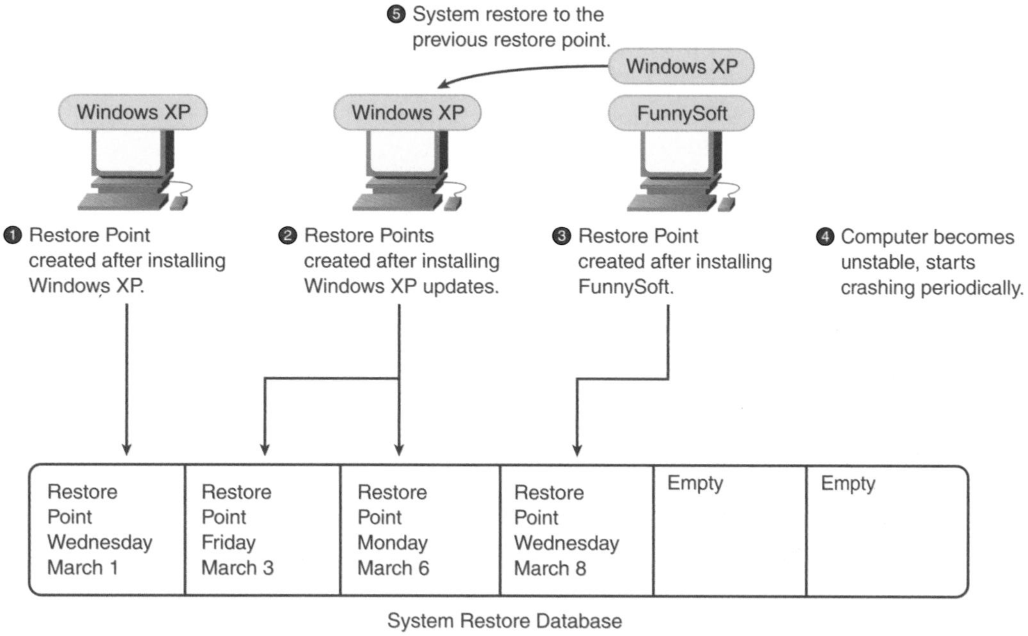

We perform some automatic updates on March 3 and 6. Each time, a new restore point is automatically added to the system restore database by Windows XP.

On March 8, we install a software program called FunnySoft. Just as in the past, Windows creates a new restore point. However, this time, our computer starts acting funny and starts periodically crashing. We suspect that the FunnySoft program is the culprit and try to uninstall it, but the computer remains somewhat unstable.

To attempt another remedy, we can go to the System Restore function in Windows XP and revert the computer back to a previous restore point, such as March 6 (when we knew it was working well), effectively undoing the changes made since then.

For all intents and purposes, Windows is returned to the point before the FunnySoft program was installed.

VERY IMPORTANT: **Keep in mind that System Restore does not remove the program files from the hard disk; it only reverts the operating system files and Windows system registry to a previous point. It also does not remove any of your own files from any directories, only operating system files.**

Creating a Restore Point

Restore points are created automatically anytime you install new software or otherwise significantly alter the computer's configuration. Sometimes you might have a well-functioning computer, such as after you have done some installations, cleanup, and so on, when you want to manually create an ideal restore point.

The steps are easy:

Step 1   Click **Start > All Programs > Accessories > System Tools > System Restore**. The main System Restore dialog will appear, as shown in Figure 4-8.

Step 2   Click the **Create a restore point** button and click **Next**.

Step 3   You can add a name for the restore point so that you can more easily recognize it if you need to find it. In this example, we name it "good restore point," as shown in Figure 4-9. Click **Create**.

Figure 4-8   System Restore Utility

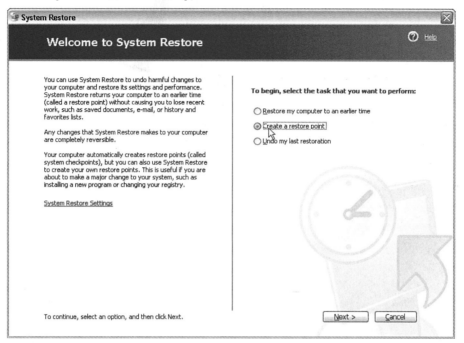

Figure 4-9   Creating a Restore Point

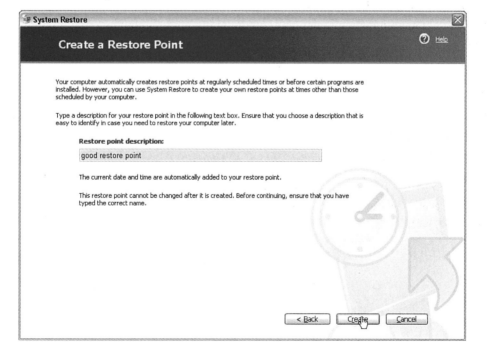

Step 4 Windows then creates the requested restore point and confirms its creation, as shown in Figure 4-10.

Figure 4-10 Restore Point Created

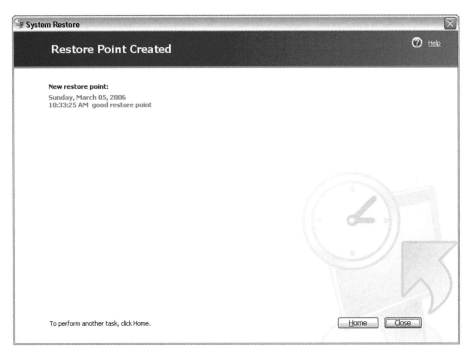

Now at any point after this "good" point in time, if we mess up the computer inadvertently, we can return the computer to this well-functioning point.

Restoring Your Computer to a Restore Point

Restoring your computer to a previous "save" point is just as easy:

Step 1 As before, access System Restore by clicking **Start > All Programs > Accessories > System Tools > System Restore**. The main System Restore dialog will appear, as shown in Figure 4-11.

Step 2 Select **Restore my computer to an earlier time** and click **Next**.

Step 3 Using the Calendar, as shown in Figure 4-12, select the restore point you want to go back to and click **Next**. The days in bold font indicate days with restore points. You can then select on the right which restore point that day, if there is more than one.

Step 4 System Restore confirms that you want to restore the computer to the selected restore point, as shown in Figure 4-13. Click **Next** to confirm (or **Cancel** if you change your mind).

Figure 4-11   Restoring to a Previous Restore Point

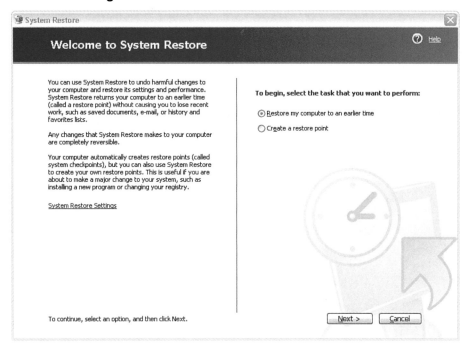

Figure 4-12   Selecting the Restore Point You Want to Restore To

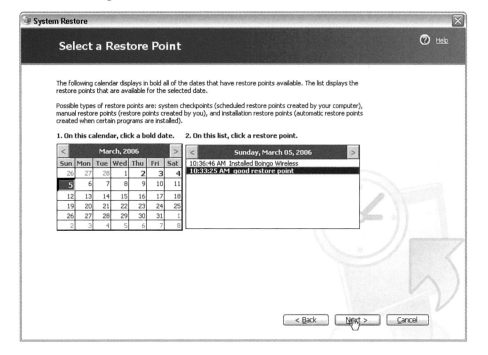

Figure 4-13   Confirming You Want to Restore

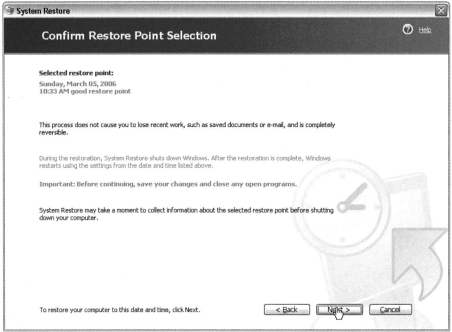

Windows then restores the computer to the selected restore point but needs to reboot to complete the task. After the restore and reboot are completed, any changes made to the computer beyond the restore point are undone.

VERY IMPORTANT: **System Restore and Windows restore points only deal with system files. They have nothing to do with backing up, preserving, or undoing changes made to personal files, such as Microsoft Word documents or Excel spreadsheets. You** *cannot* **undo any action to such files by restoring your computer to a previous restore point.**

What to Do If You Think Your Operating System Has Been Compromised

If you think your operating system has been compromised or corrupted, either through an inadvertent action on your part or perhaps by a computer virus infection, you can take some steps to try and recover.

The first action is to recognize that something is wrong. In some cases, it might be fairly subtle, and you will not necessarily notice anything wrong. In other cases, it will be painfully obvious that something major is wrong. Table 4-1 lists a few common problems related to virus infections (some of these could also indicate a physical hard drive failure).

Table 4-1   Common Virus-Related Errors

Windows Error Message	Probable Cause
Windows XP could not start because the following file is missing or corrupt: \WINDOWS\SYSTEM32\CONFIG\SYSTEM	System registry is corrupted or destroyed.
Stop: c0000218 {Registry File Failure} The registry cannot load the hive (file): \SystemRoot\System32\Config\SOFTWARE or its log or alternate	System registry is corrupted or destroyed.
Invalid partition table	Corrupted or missing boot sector.
Error loading operating system	Corrupted or missing boot sector.
Missing operating system	Corrupted or missing boot sector.
BOOT: Couldn't find NTLDR	Corrupted or missing boot sector.
STOP: 0x0000007B (*parameter1*, *parameter2*, *parameter3*, *parameter4*) INACCESSIBLE_BOOT_DEVICE	Corrupted or missing boot sector.
Windows File Protection Files that are required for Windows to run properly have been replaced by unrecognized versions. To maintain system stability, Windows must restore the original versions of these files. Insert your *product* CD-ROM now.	Operating system files have been replaced or corrupted.

If you do seem to have a major issue, you can attempt to remedy the problem several ways. The recommended steps are as follows:

Step 1   Run an antivirus scan (see Chapter 3) and determine whether the antivirus program can remove and repair the problem.

Step 2   If the computer is virus free (the antivirus scan completes with no problems found), try to restore the computer to a previous restore point.

Step 3   If System Restore is not possible, or it has no effect, check and repair the Windows system files:

Click **Start > Run** and enter **sfc /scannow** in the dialog box, as shown in Figure 4-14. Click **OK**.

Figure 4-14   Running the Windows XP System File Check

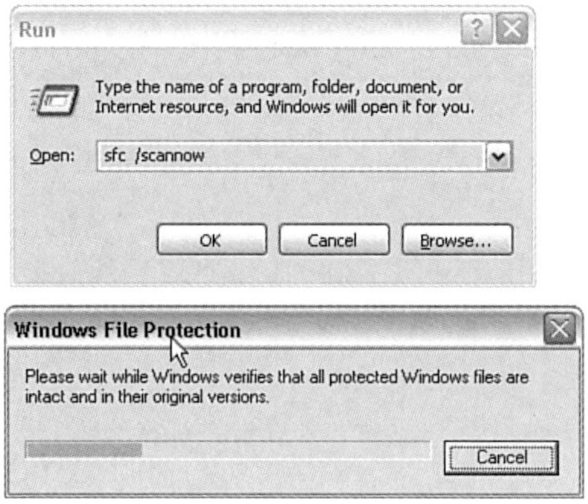

The Windows XP *System File Check* (SFC) utility will examine all the Windows system files on your computer. If it detects corrupted or missing files, it will replace them with the original correct files. It can take 20 to 30 minutes or so to finish, so be patient. You might need your original Windows XP installation CD handy because you might not have all the proper utility files loaded on your computer; in which case, you will be prompted for files that are on that CD.

Step 4   It might be necessary to reload the Windows operating system from the installation CD.

Step 5   Check for recommendations on the specific issue and error message that is appearing, by consulting the Microsoft website:

http://support.microsoft.com/

Summary

Keeping your Windows operating system current will not solve all security issues in your home network. However, it is an important step to keep as many potential security holes closed as possible so that the fewest number of potential flaws (that might be exploited) exist on your computer.

Keep the rest of the software programs on your computer updated for the same reasons.

As a final note, it will be invaluable for you to have the data on your computer backed up to an external drive or some other backup. If all goes wrong and you have to reload the computer from scratch, you will thank yourself for spending the time to do so. Backups are covered in detail in Chapter 9, "Tip 9: Back Up Your Files."

Where to Go for More Information

You can find more information about updating your operating system and restore points at the following websites:

http://www.microsoft.com/athome/security/protect/update.mspx

http://www.microsoft.com/technet/prodtechnol/winxppro/support/restore.mspx

CHAPTER 5

Tip 5: Lock Out Spyware and Adware

Threat Type: Software based, victim enabled

Examples of Threats:

- Popping up advertisements all over your computer screen

- Installing programs to collect and report data on your Internet browsing habits

- Inserting toolbar or searchbar programs into your browser or applications, such as Internet Explorer, which slow down your computer's performance

- Collecting and reporting information about which websites you visit so that you can be targeted more effectively with advertisements and marketing

Our Tips:

- Install and enable a popup blocker.

- Install and enable a spyware/adware blocker.

- Use a personal firewall program on each computer to prevent unauthorized program installations and Internet access (see Chapter 1, "Tip 1: Use Firewalls").

- Avoid downloading "free" software programs that have strings attached.

- Periodically use a spyware elimination program to find and delete spyware and adware.

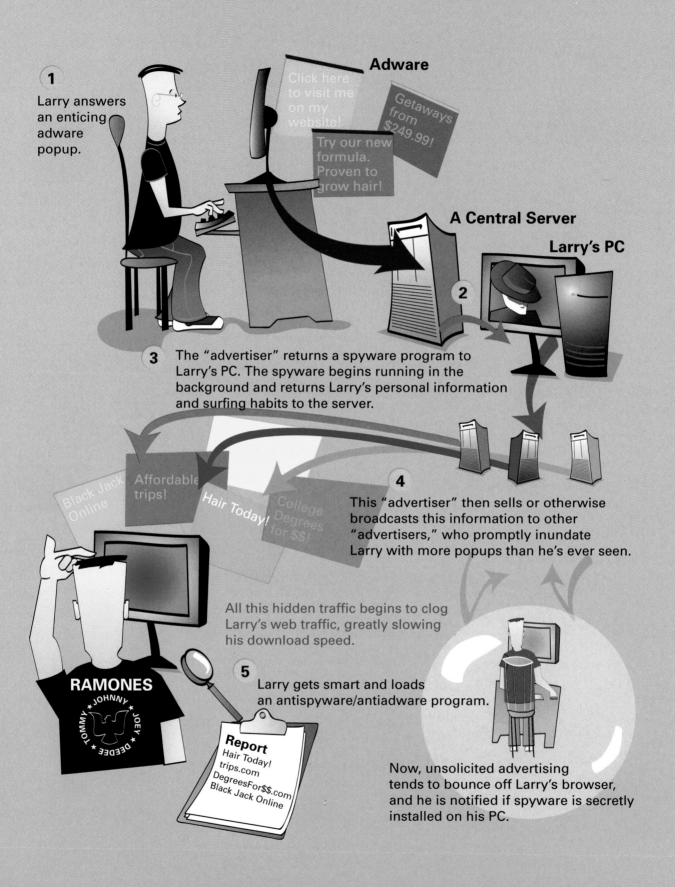

1

Larry answers an enticing adware popup.

Adware

Click here to visit me on my website!

Getaways from $249.99!

Try our new formula. Proven to grow hair!

A Central Server

Larry's PC

2

3 The "advertiser" returns a spyware program to Larry's PC. The spyware begins running in the background and returns Larry's personal information and surfing habits to the server.

Black Jack Online

Affordable trips!

Hair Today!

College Degrees for $$!

4

This "advertiser" then sells or otherwise broadcasts this information to other "advertisers," who promptly inundate Larry with more popups than he's ever seen.

All this hidden traffic begins to clog Larry's web traffic, greatly slowing his download speed.

RAMONES
JOHNNY ★ JOEY ★ DEEDEE ★ TOMMY

Report
Hair Today!
trips.com
DegreesFor$$.com
Black Jack Online

5 Larry gets smart and loads an antispyware/antiadware program.

Now, unsolicited advertising tends to bounce off Larry's browser, and he is notified if spyware is secretly installed on his PC.

One of the engines that has driven the explosive growth of the Internet is the concept of eyeballs. For a relatively low price, you are provided with a high-speed broadband connection that gives you access to an endless amount of mostly free information, services, digital media, and even software programs.

Ever ask yourself how these companies stay in business? For example, how does Weather.com pay their bills to be able to bring you awesome up-to-the-minute radar images for your city's weather? How can people give you software programs such as screensavers and games for free?

The answer is eyeballs. *Eyeballs* refers to the number of people's eyes someone can get to view their Internet content (and accompanying advertisements). Yes, the Internet is based on relatively the same concept as commercial television.

The difference is the Internet can bring highly targeted advertising like never before and sometimes nearly force you to view it. Banner and popup ads were the first wave, but most people are tuning them out, so to speak, by installing popup blockers. So, advertisers are relying on more sophisticated methods to get their stuff in front of your eyes.

An all-out brawl is looming between consumers and advertisers. Between cable networks, DVRs, and TiVo players, we can screen out quite a few commercials. With increasingly good technology, we can also screen out a lot of advertisements online, too, which is the focus of the rest of this chapter.

What Is Spyware and Adware?

So, why spyware and adware? Well, quite frankly, online advertisers are getting more desperate to keep the ads under your nose. As a result, there is an escalation of techniques occurring, some getting pretty aggressive. These techniques include adware and spyware.

Adware

There is not one agreed upon definition of what *adware* is and is not, but in general it includes any program used to facilitate getting advertising content in front of you on your computer, including the following:

- **Popups**—Advertisements that pop up on your computer screen as new windows, especially while you are browsing the Internet.

- **Adware**—Although the whole category of advertisements is often referred to as adware, the term also is used in reference to hidden programs inside of other programs. This is usually from free software or a game you download that is permitted to shower you with ads as the price you pay for using it for free.

- **Annoyware**—Term for aggressive adware practices, such as asking whether you want to install a program and then only allowing you to click OK and not Cancel, or popups that when you close them keep popping up more and more additional ones.

- **Banner ads**—Blending an advertisement into a website in an official-looking banner, enticing you to click it because you think it is part of the page you are browsing.

- **Drive-by downloads**—Suddenly asking you to download a program that you did not ask for while browsing the Internet.

- **Warning boxes**—Making a popup ad look like a typical warning box you get in Windows. Our favorites are those that claim your system is infected with adware/spyware and then try to sell you an antiadware program. Adware selling antiadware. Beautiful.

Most adware is obtained willingly, by you agreeing to see advertisements for using a free piece of software or service on a website. You probably do not even notice this in the fine print of the user agreement when you click the Accept button. (Adware vendors are counting on the fact that you don't.)

Spyware

There is also not one agreed upon definition of what *spyware* is and is not, but in general it includes any program used to gather and relay information from your computer to a location collecting the information, including the following:

- **Data miners**—Actively collect information from you and then relay it to a remote server.

- **Spyware**—As in the adware case, this term is used for both the category and for a particular instance within the category. In this case, we are referring to a hidden program that collects information and sends it to a central server without your knowledge or consent.

- **Trackware**—Generally passive method of tracking with cookies what site or sites you have visited and also some amount of personal information.

- **Hijacker**—These little gems like to hijack your Internet Explorer settings, such as changing your home page to where they want you to go or hijacking and overlaying the search function.

- **Searchbars and toolbars**—Toolbars for searching that can be added as add-ons to Internet Explorer. They generally cause slow performance on your computer and can be used to track what information you search for and browse.

Some spyware is obtained willingly, by you agreeing to participate in some trial marketing for using a free piece of software or service on a website. Just as often, you might think you are agreeing to adware when in reality a program has been placed on your computer that can collect information and send it to a marketing company.

Figure 5-1 shows an example of spyware. In this example, the spyware program is put in a popup ad as a payload. When the computer user clicks the popup ad, the spyware program is deposited on the computer.

After the initial deposit, the spyware can track whatever it was created for (for example, which applications are running on the PC or which web pages are browsed most often). Periodically, the spyware can call home, by sending its information to the creating company over the Internet.

Figure 5-1   How Spyware Works

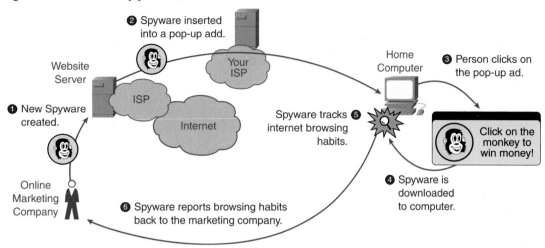

Are Spyware and Adware Viruses?

Although many adware and spyware programs increasingly share some of the characteristics of viruses, especially stealth and doing things without your knowledge, the primary distinction is that viruses live to replicate, whereas spyware and adware live to gather information that can be sent to marketing companies or to entice you to buy a specific product.

In general, spyware and adware are a one-to-one relationship between you and whatever marketing organization is trying to sell you stuff. They generally do not replicate themselves and send themselves to other computers. Spyware and adware tend to operate more on the "cow pattie" model: meaning they lie around on websites until you step in one, and then they cling to your shoe until you can shake them loose.

Preventing Spyware and Adware

Adware is mainly an annoyance but can slow down the performance of you computer. Spyware is a larger threat because it can be an invasion of your privacy. You can take four steps to remedy the threat:

- Exercise common sense.

- Block popups.

- Install an antispyware/antiadware program.

- Implement a personal software firewall.

The first three are covered in the sections that follow. Personal software firewalls are covered in Chapter 1.

Exercising Common Sense

The easiest way to avoid dealing with spyware and adware on your computer is the same as for viruses: Do not get them in the first place. Easier said than done, but here are some tips:

- Avoid downloading "free" software programs, screensavers, and any program that comes with strings attached.

- If you are not sure whether there are strings attached, do some quick Internet research on the software program.

- Do not click on popup ads, even to win money from a monkey.

- Do not fall for popups on your computer saying your computer is infected with spyware.

- Ask yourself why something of value is being offered for free. What do they have to gain from giving it to you?

It is almost impossible never to get adware or spyware on your computer. Just like viruses, we have had them, and everyone we know has had them.

Installing a Popup Blocker

The first step in avoiding adware and spyware (and to save yourself a ton of annoyance) is to turn on a popup blocker to stop the endless stream of windows with advertisements popping up on your computer screen while you are on the Internet. You have a couple of options.

Turning On the Internet Explorer Built-In Popup Blocker

If you are running Windows XP Service Pack 2 (SP2), you have a popup blocker already. All you need to do is turn it on. If your version of XP is not SP2, you can acquire it here:

http://www.microsoft.com/windowsxp/sp2/default.mspx

The popup blocker is built in to Internet Explorer. To turn it on, click **Tools > Pop-up Blocker > Turn On Pop-up Blocker**, as shown in Figure 5-2.

That was easy. Periodically, some websites might use popups you want to see, not as ads but as part of the way that website functions to show you information. You can just toggle the popup blocker in your browser off temporarily. Just remember to turn it back on when you leave that website.

When you turn on the popup blocker, the menu option will change to **Tools > Pop-up Blocker > Turn Off Pop-up Blocker**. You just use the same menu option to toggle the feature on and off.

Installing a Third-Party Popup Blocker Program

If you do not have Windows XP (still running Windows 98SE, 2000, or ME), you do not have the option to upgrade Internet Explorer to receive the built-in popup blocker.

However, several popup blockers are available for free (yes, we know we said not to download free stuff). Pop-Up Stopper from Panicware is a pretty decent one. You can get it here:

http://www.panicware.com/product_psfree.html

Figure 5-2   Enabling the Internet Explorer Popup Blocker

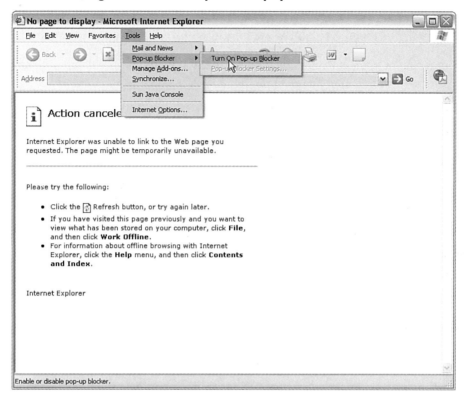

After you install it, a little white glove icon will appear in the lower right of your screen (on the running tasks bar). If you double-click the glove, you can toggle Pop-Up Stopper on and off, as shown in Figure 5-3.

Figure 5-3   Panicware Pop-Up Stopper

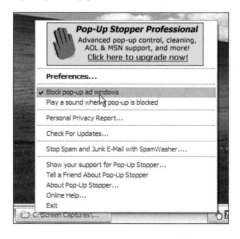

If the glove is white, Pop-Up Stopper is on. If the glove is "empty" (no color), Pop-Up Stopper is off.

Installing an Antispyware/Antiadware Program

The next step in adware and spyware prevention is to install an antispyware/antiadware program. Figure 5-4 shows how these programs work. They work similarly to antivirus programs.

Figure 5-4   How Antispyware/Antiadware Works

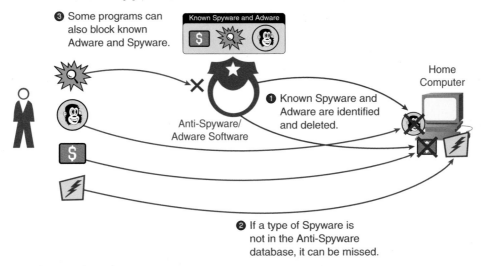

Your computer is scanned for known spyware and adware programs, matching them against a list of known spyware/adware signatures. If detected, you can remove them. If a piece of spyware is not yet in the signature list, it will be missed, again similar to antivirus.

Also similar to antivirus, but not quite there yet in terms of technology (that is, it is pretty new at the time of publication), is the ability to do active scanning, meaning blocking the insertion of adware and spyware into your computer in the first place. This is preferable rather than detecting and deleting it, after it is already on your computer and operating.

You have several options for antispyware/antiadware programs, including the following:

■ Installing a freeware program from the Internet

■ Installing Windows Defender, a relatively new option

■ Enabling the antispyware/antiadware function in a security bundle you already own or plan to buy

The following sections look at each option. Any option will work, but they do have different advantages and disadvantages, so weigh which one is right for you. You might want to install all of them and then pick which one is right for you. Multiple programs for scanning are okay. However, be careful having multiple programs setup for active scanning at the same time because it could affect your computer's performance.

Free Antispyware/Antiadware Programs

A couple of really good antispyware/antiadware programs are available on the Internet for free. If you have been paying attention at all, you should be saying, "Hey, you told me not to do that." Well, exceptions apply to every rule.

The basic version of these programs is free. They make money by offering an upgrade to a premium version that has more features and a higher level of service. We look at the basic versions here.

Spybot Search & Destroy

The first is a product called Spybot Search & Destroy from Safer Networking. It is available here for download:

> http://www.safer-networking.org/

After installing the program, you can double-click the desktop icon to start it. You will see a dialog like Figure 5-5.

Figure 5-5   Spybot Search & Destroy Main Control Panel

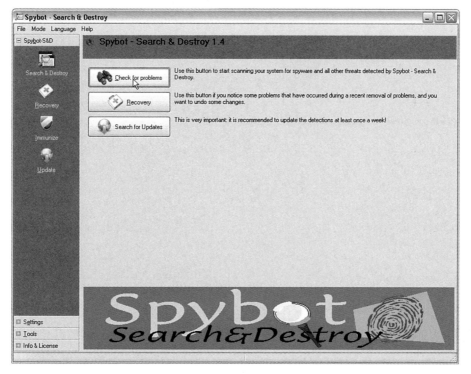

Clicking **Search for Updates** downloads the latest signatures over the Internet to your computer so that Spybot has the latest set of spyware/adware knowledge to search with.

Clicking **Check for problems** scans your computer for known spyware and adware problems. When the scan has completed, you will see a display such as Figure 5-6, showing the spyware and adware programs that were detected on your computer.

Figure 5-6   Spybot Scan Completed and Spyware/Adware Detected

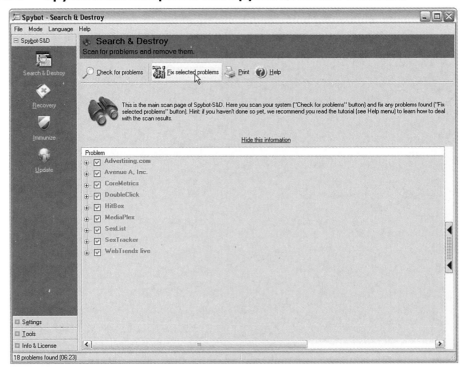

Clicking **Fix selected problems** removes all the spyware and adware programs that are checked.

VERY IMPORTANT: Some adware programs are on your computer because you downloaded something, such as a screensaver program, that you are using for free under the agreement that the adware can live on your computer and bring you advertisements. If you remove the adware with Spybot or any other tool, you will likely disrupt the freebie program you are using. So, if you want to keep a particular piece of adware, uncheck it in the list before you click Fix selected problems.

Spybot attempts to remove the selected adware and spyware programs and gives you a report about whether it succeeded, as shown in Figure 5-7.

That's it, pretty easy, but you do have to remember to perform a scan periodically.

VERY IMPORTANT: Adware and spyware scans have to search a lot of files on your hard disk; so, depending how large your disk is, how many files you have, how fast your computer is, and how many adware and spyware signatures the program needs to look for, it can take several minutes to complete a scan.

Figure 5-7   Spybot Removes Spyware/Adware

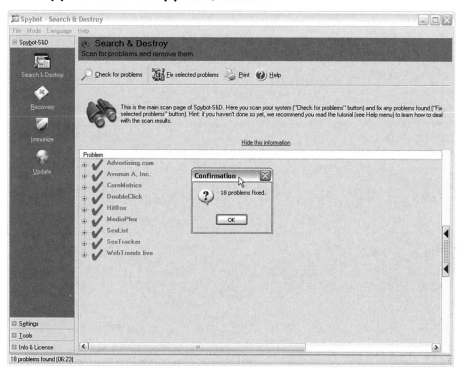

If you would rather automate when scans occur, you can do that, too. Follow these steps:

Step 1   Click the **Mode > Advanced** option on the toolbar to turn on the more advanced functions of Spybot Search & Destroy.

Step 2   Click the **Settings** plus sign on the left side of the control window. Then, click **Settings** below that. Page down in the panel on the right of the window to a section called Automation, as shown in Figure 5-8.

Step 3   Under System start, select the following options:

- **Automatically run program at system startup.**

- **Run check on program start.**

- **Fix all problems on program start.**

- **Wait a few minutes until starting the check.**

- **Close program if everything's O.K.**

Step 4   Under Web update, select the following options:

- **Search the web for new versions at each program start.**

- **Download updated include files if available online.**

Step 5   Click **File > Exit** to save the settings.

Figure 5-8 Spybot Settings for Automated Scanning

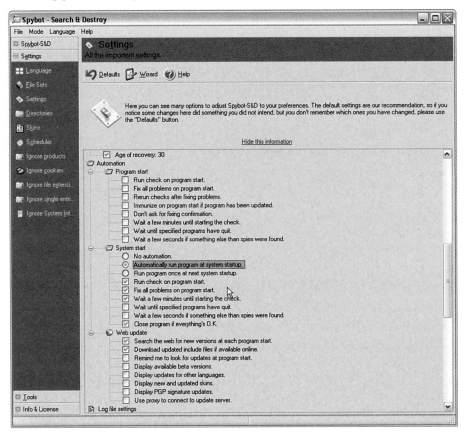

Now, each time Windows is started, Spybot will automatically start, download the latest adware/
spyware signatures, and start scanning. The scanning looks slightly different, as shown in Figure 5-9.
Because many different programs compete for the CPU resources as the computer starts up, it is a
good idea to set the startup time to about 4 or 5 minutes after Windows boots.

Figure 5-9 Spybot Auto-Scanning After Windows Boot

When the scan completes, Spybot automatically removes any detected spyware and adware.

Spybot Search & Destroy is a pretty good antispyware/antiadware program. It is mainly a "sweeper," meaning it scans and removes spyware programs after they are already there. A few prevention features are starting to appear in Spybot. Check out the Immunize function.

Finally, the good folks at Safer Networking operate today based on donations. So, if you like Spybot Search & Destroy, consider kicking a few euros their way (they are based in Ireland).

Ad-Aware

The next product to consider is called Ad-Aware from Lavasoft (a Swedish company; apparently Europeans hate adware and spyware even more than Americans).

It is fairly similar to Spybot, in that it is a "sweeper" type of program. The basic (personal) version is free, with a more enhanced version available for a small fee. One of the features available in the pay version is Ad-Watch, which offers spyware/adware prevention and blocking before it reaches your computer. Both versions are available here:

    http://www.lavasoft.com/

After you have installed Ad-Aware, you can access the Ad-Aware main control window by double-clicking the desktop icon. It looks like Figure 5-10.

Figure 5-10   Ad-Aware Main Control Window

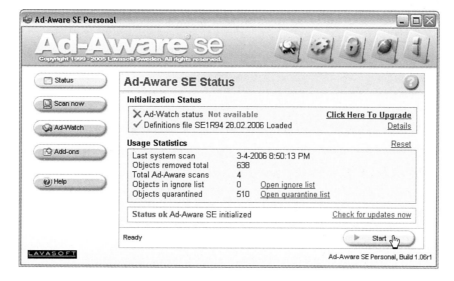

Clicking **Check for updates now** checks for and downloads the latest signatures from the web. Clicking **Scan now** triggers a full system scan against the known adware and spyware signatures. When it completes, you receive a report like that shown in Figure 5-11.

To remove any detected items, click **Next** and follow the instructions.

Ad-Aware is another pretty good product. If you try it and like it, consider upgrading to the pay version to get the prevention component, Ad-Watch.

Figure 5-11 Ad-Aware Scan Completed and Spyware/Adware Detected

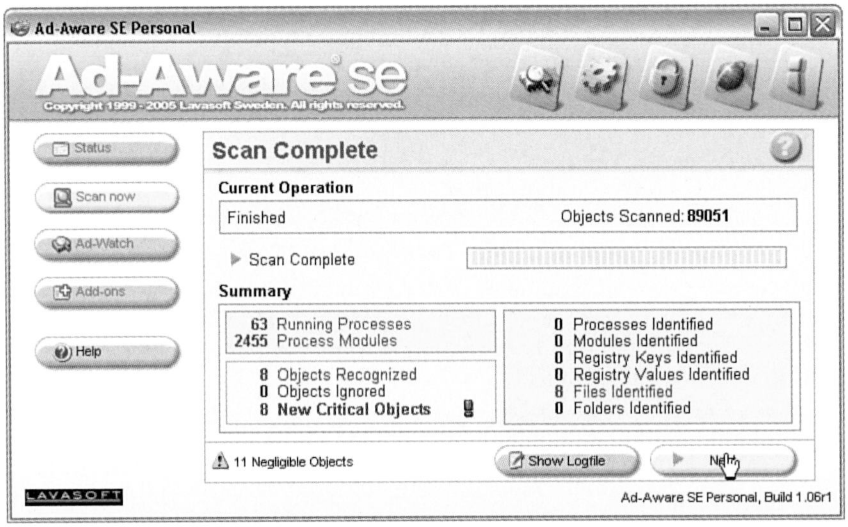

Windows Defender

The next option to consider is called Windows Defender (beta 2), formerly known as Windows AntiSpyware (beta). Defender is a beta version (at the time of this writing) of antispyware/antiadware from Microsoft that integrates with Windows. (Beta means it is still undergoing testing, but you can use it at your own risk.)

Defender can run on Windows XP SP2 and later (or Windows 2000 SP4 and later). It offers both detection (passive scanning) and prevention (active scanning). Windows Defender (beta) is free for Windows users (at the time of this writing).

See the following website to download and try Defender:

http://www.microsoft.com/athome/security/spyware/software

After you install Defender, you will see a little gray castle icon running on your taskbar and a corresponding desktop icon. Defender automatically starts every time Windows starts up and stays running in the background. The main Defender control window looks like Figure 5-12.

A green status means no threats have been detected. You can adjust some of the settings by clicking **Tools > General Settings**, as shown in Figure 5-13.

Some of the recommended settings you want to checkmark are these:

- **Automatically scan my computer** (and you specify the frequency, daily or weekly are recommended, and time of day)

- **Check for updated definitions before scanning**

- **Apply actions on detected items after scanning**

Figure 5-12   Windows Defender Main Status Window

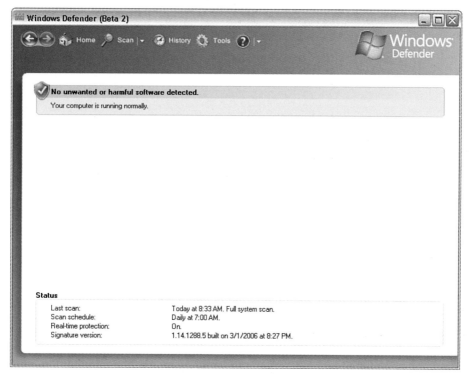

Figure 5-13   Windows Defender Settings

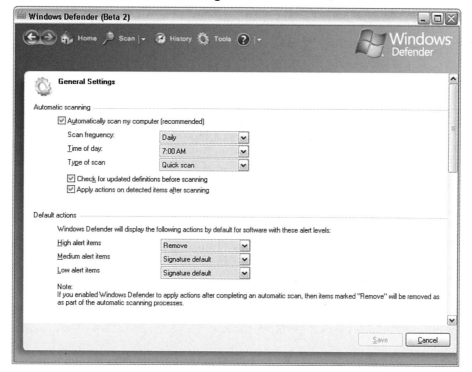

With these settings enabled, Defender will always automatically get the latest adware and spyware signatures over the Internet, and scan your computer periodically. If a problem is found, you will see a red status appear, as shown in Figure 5-14.

Figure 5-14   Windows Defender Detects a Problem

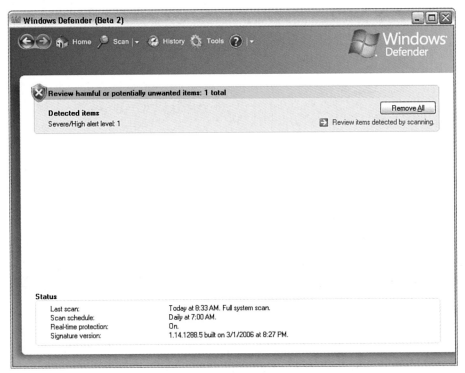

Clicking the warning area takes you to a page where you can manually determine what you want to do with the spyware or adware detected, as shown in Figure 5-15.

The Action options are **Ignore**, **Remove**, or **Allow**. Unless you need it, select **Remove** and then **Apply Actions**. Alternatively, click **Remove All** if you want to get rid of all of it.

Figure 5-16 shows a list of adware that has been removed by Defender.

Figure 5-15   Windows Defender Requests What to Do with Detected Spyware

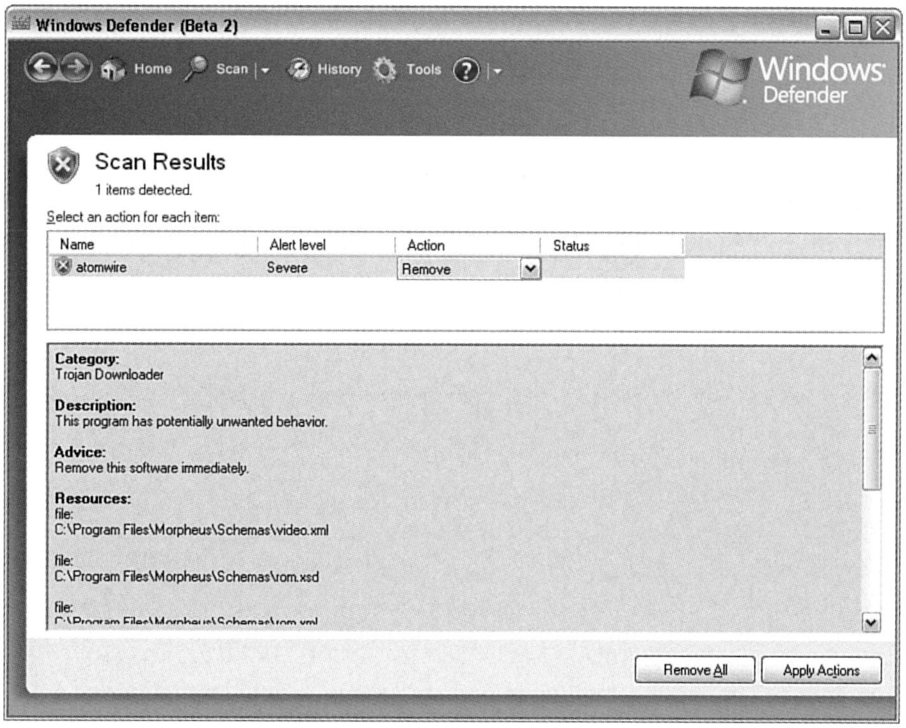

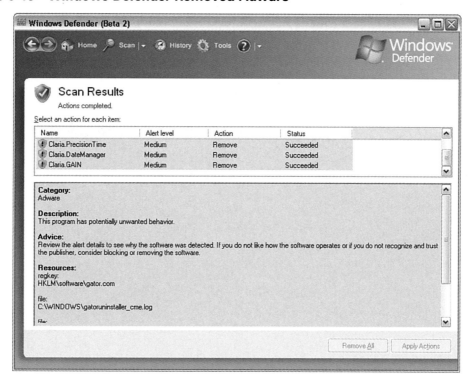

Figure 5-16   Windows Defender Removed Adware

That covers the passive scanning mode of Defender (meaning detecting, and removing spyware/adware when it is already there). Let's now look at Defender's active scanning to see how it can help prevent spyware/adware from being installed in the first place.

Windows Defender runs in the background on your computer. If you click something to install that has spyware or adware associated with it, Defender pops up a warning, such as the example shown in Figure 5-17.

Figure 5-17   Windows Defender Adware/Spyware Warning

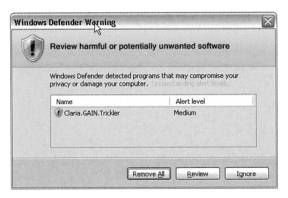

You can then avoid installing the software and thereby prevent the adware from getting on your computer. Another cool feature of Defender is the ability to report potential spyware threats back to Microsoft for investigation (so that future versions of Defender can be improved with the latest signatures).

Windows Defender (still in beta, do not forget, but could be production-ready by the time you read this book) seems like a pretty good addition to Windows for security. Adding to that Windows Firewall and Windows Live OneCare antivirus, and it would seem that Microsoft is finally on their way to incorporating much needed security into Windows.

Antispyware/Antiadware in the Security Bundles

A final option available for antispyware/antiadware is that if you decided to buy or already own one of the security software bundles (such as McAfee Internet Security Suite 200x, Symantec Norton Internet Security 200x, Trend Micro PC-cillin Internet Security, or ZoneAlarm Internet Security Suite), all have an antispyware/antiadware component.

See Table 1-1 (Chapter 1) or Table 3-1 (Chapter 3) for the location of the websites to purchase one of the security bundle products.

For these products, consult the User Guide for how to enable the spyware/adware protection.

Figure 5-18 shows one example for enabling antispyware/antiadware in Symantec's product.

Figure 5-18   Turning On Spyware/Adware Blocking with Symantec Norton Internet Security 200x

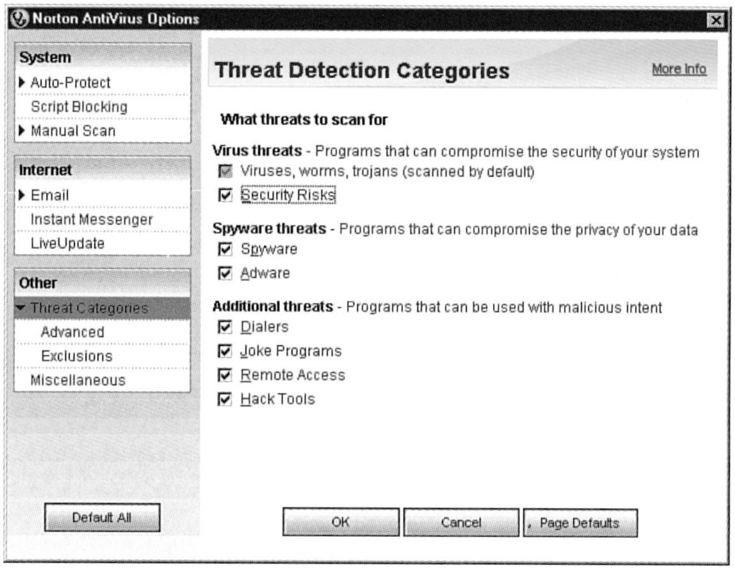

What to Do If You Think You've Been Infected

If you think your computer might already be infected with spyware or adware, you are probably correct. If you have never performed a spyware/adware scan before, chances are pretty good you have some.

Some symptoms of spyware/adware can include the following:

- New toolbars or searchbars appearing in your Internet browser
- New programs that you do not recognize appearing in your add/remove programs list
- Sluggish computer performance
- Popup ads that keep appearing

One way to see what is happening in your computer is to check out the running tasks list. In Windows XP, you can press the **Ctrl-Alt-Del** keys simultaneously and then click **Task Manager**. First check the **Performance** tab, which shows you what percentage of your computer's processor is being used over time. If it is excessively high, you could have spyware/adware consuming cycles.

If you do think you have spyware and adware on your computer, you can take a number of steps to remove them.

Spyware/Adware-Removal Tools

The first option is the antispyware/antiadware programs discussed earlier in this chapter. All the options presented scan your computer and detect known adware and spyware programs (and remove them).

Some adware and spyware will not be completely removable by these tools and might be more stubborn to eradicate.

Removing Spyware and Adware Programs Using the Installed Programs List

If you run across stubborn adware or spyware that cannot be completely removed by the antispyware/antiadware program you are using, you might have to remove the program using the Windows Add/Remove Programs panel.

To do so, click **Start > Control Panel > Add/Remove Programs**. As shown in Figure 5-19, click the program you want to remove, and then click **Change/Remove**.

Figure 5-19   Uninstalling an Unwanted Program

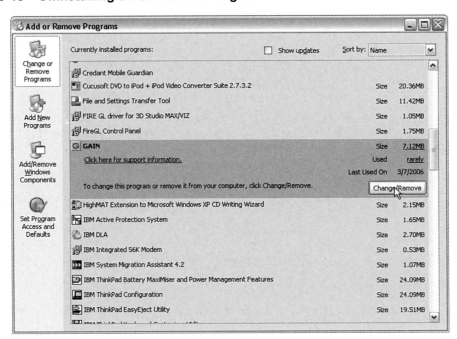

The adware program will be uninstalled. Often, as part of the uninstall process, the adware or spyware will open the Internet browser, go to their website, and ask you to confirm you want to delete it. They will also typically pester you a bit with questions about why you are uninstalling.

In general, it is good practice to become familiar with the programs in the Add/Remove Programs list (and the Program Control list in your personal software firewall). That way, when a new entry unexpectedly appears, you can recognize it.

If you are not sure whether the program is adware/spyware or a legitimate program, the best thing to do is look in the directory under C: /Program Files and get the name of the .exe or .dll file. Then search on the name at one of these online resources:

http://www.pcpitstop.com/spycheck/known.asp

http://www.processlibrary.com

They will tell you whether the program files are spyware/adware or legitimate.

Some adware, spyware, and viruses will not be detected by antispyware/antiadware/antivirus software and will not show up in the Add/Remove Programs list or in your program files. These will be more difficult to remove, and the multitude of possibilities here requires detail no book has room for. If you suspect you have spyware, adware, or a virus and the steps covered previously do not get rid of the symptoms or the problem, you will have to do a bit of research. Go to a trusted security discussion forum and post details about the symptoms or problems you are having. Chances are someone out there has discovered a way to fix the same problem you are having and will share some steps to help you. Remember, only follow steps from a trusted site, such as the support forum at your security product's website.

Summary

Popup blockers are a good first step toward protecting against spyware/adware programs finding their way onto your computer.

Antispyware/antiadware programs offer protection against most spyware and adware threats. Some programs provide passive scanning (detection after infection), whereas others provide both passive and active scanning (detection before infection).

Much like antivirus technology, antispyware/antiadware programs rely on regular updates of signatures to be effective.

Where to Go for More Information

You can learn more about spyware/adware from the following websites:

http://www.microsoft.com/athome/security/spyware

http://www.lavasoft.com/trackware_info

http://www.safer-networking.org/en/tutorial.

CHAPTER 6

Tip 6: Keep an Eye on Your Kids

Threat Type: Victim enabled

Examples of Threats:

- Children accidentally or intentionally gaining access to adult content on the Internet, including pornography, graphic images or language, gambling, and so forth

- Children being contacted by predators in online chat rooms or blogging sites

- Parents held accountable for illegal activities conducted by their children, such as hacking or illegal file sharing

- Excessive use by children of the Internet without parental knowledge

Our Tips:

- Discuss Internet use policies openly with your children and set expectations.

- Talk to your kids about the dangers of online predators contacting them.

- Advise your kids to place no personal information about themselves online; review their websites and blog sites.

- Place computers in family common areas in the house.

- Install some form of parental controls on your Internet connection, either at the ISP, home router, or on each computer.

If you have children and access to the Internet, you need to educate and arm yourself to protect them against the many dangers that they can and likely will encounter. The Internet is a particular danger to children because often the kids know more about the technology than the parents. This leads to situations where the parent is either unaware of the dangers or where the parent takes some steps to protect the children, which are easily circumvented by a tech-savvy kid.

The natural curiosity and rebellious nature of kids, combined with greater technical knowledge, means parents are at a disadvantage. Unlike other forms of rebellion, such as partying in the basement or sneaking out at night, you do not have the benefit of having tried these tricks and getting caught by your parents. The Internet is an entirely new game, and your children are the first generation of kids to have access to it.

Set rules and expectations about appropriate Internet usage with your kids. Take the time to understand how kids use the Internet and where the dangers are.

Only allow your children to use the Internet in a common area of the house and in full view of an adult.

Set rules for when children can use the Internet. These rules can be enforced with parental controls that you can set and monitor.

Your time is up. Thanks for visiting the Internet.

Beep beep.

Install child protection software to ensure that sites you don't approve of are not visited.

If a child does not follow the rules or finds ways around protection software, you can install programs that monitor and record all activity on a PC. These programs can be controlled remotely.

This chapter outlines some of the dangers or inappropriate web activity kids might encounter and steps that you can take to protect them.

What Are the Dangers Your Kids Might Encounter Online?

We keep talking about dangers. What exactly are we talking about? The next sections outline some of them.

Pornography

The number-one Internet concern for many parents (and spouses) is easy access to websites containing sexually explicit or graphically violent material. How do you tell whether your child has been somewhere he or she shouldn't be? Read on.

VERY IMPORTANT: **A rule of thumb: If kids are under 12 or so, most of the time they access adult content by accidentally clicking the wrong link or ad. If you find that teenagers have accessed an adult site, however, it is time to start asking them questions.**

Predators

One of the most frightening dangers on the Internet is the possibility of a child being contacted and then stalked by sexual predators who roam chat rooms. A favorite tactic used by predators is to pose as another kid and then lure the victim into a private chat room. There is also a danger that a child can inadvertently provide a sexual predator with personal information, such as home address, school name, phone number, or parents' work schedule. Take it seriously and report it if you find out this is happening. Sexually enticing a minor online is a crime.

By the way, a website called Perverted Justice (http://www.perverted-justice.com) tracks online sexual predators (this website is only intended for adults). The site posts their names, addresses, pictures, and sends the log files to local and federal authorities.

Gambling

There are tens of thousands of gambling sites on the Internet, both legal and illegal. Whether legitimate or a scam site, it is doubtful that most parents would allow their underage kids to visit gambling sites. There are some reports of kids "borrowing" their parents' credit card and racking up serious debt in no time at all. If this happens, parents might actually be liable for the charges their children run up.

Hacking

We mentioned hacker programs that reside inside other, often "free" or shareware programs. Kids tend to be more vulnerable than adults because most do not have the financial wherewithal to purchase software programs on their own; instead, they are more likely to download freeware from the Internet. Be suspicious of any free program targeted at children.

Another issue to be aware of is your children turning into amateur hackers themselves. An Internet community called "script kiddies," referring to rather amateur, script-driven hacking, easily attracts smart yet bored kids. Hacking might not look like an immediate danger to your family; however, it is illegal and, therefore, you can be held liable for any damages done by your child.

Illegal Peer-to-Peer Sharing

Peer-to-peer sites are often used to illegally trade copyrighted material. In addition to being a favorite cover for people distributing viruses and spyware, sharing copyrighted material (songs, movies, games, and so on) is punishable by law in the United States and many other countries. As with gambling sites, parents can be held financially responsible if a child is found guilty of copyright infringement. Lawsuits brought by the music industry (RIAA) against people sharing music illegally on the Internet are typically resulting in thousands of dollars per family in settlements.

Maybe I Should Rethink This Internet Thing

Now that we have scared you, you're probably thinking it might be a good idea to never ever let your kids use the Internet again. Well, that is probably not such a good idea because

- It puts them at a serious disadvantage in school and socially. The Internet is a fantastic resource of information and communication that is helping kids to excel in learning.

- If they do not use the Internet at home, they will access it somewhere else. It is too big and too easy to get access to. So it is a good thing if you are around when they do so that you can monitor and set the rules.

Given that, you can do a number of things to keep your kids out of danger—to protect children who do not know better and to prevent children (and spouses) from breaking the rules:

- **Educate yourself**—The fact that you are reading this is a big step in the right direction, but it should not end here. Keep up-to-date with new threats, scams, and solutions.

- **Browse in plain sight**—Only allow your children to be online in a common part of the house where you can see them and the computer screen by just passing by. Kids are much less likely to be lured into inappropriate websites or chat rooms if you are monitoring their online activity.

- **Explain the rules**—Make sure your kids understand the potential dangers online. Set ground rules and communicate them to your children, including consequences.

- **Use a parental control program**—Numerous programs are available that allow you to block inappropriate online content. We walk through a couple of programs that we found very useful later in this chapter.

- **Log and monitor (as a last resort)**—If you have a child (or spouse) who, despite your rules, keeps attempting to view adult material, you can buy a program that allows you to record everything that appears on a computer screen.

For all the good that the Internet provides, it can be a dangerous place for kids. For the most part, the good outweighs the bad and, although the adult sites and chat rooms and online gambling halls are fine for adults who want to visit them, you need to protect your kids from visiting them whether they simply mistype a popular web address or if their curiosity gets the best of them.

As a starting point, try these three steps. If they do not work, go on to something more restrictive:

- Move the computers to common areas, such as a kitchen or living room.

- Use a Windows program or other parental control program to put time restrictions on computer use.

- Use the built-in parental controls on a Linksys router or at your ISP.

The next few sections discuss these options and others in more detail.

Preparing Kids for Being Online

The first step to keeping your kids safe online is to prepare them. You need to both advise them of the potential dangers online and to set your expectations of what you consider to be appropriate use of the Internet and what is not. The next few sections lay out some points to consider.

Establish and Communicate the Internet Usage Policy

As a parent, you need to decide what Internet usage framework you are going to provide for your child. Some things are pretty clear cut (for example, blocking access to pornography). But, there are gray areas, such as medical or biology sites and graphic news reports.

Time limits also seem straightforward, just limit to one hour a day and never between the hours of 10 p.m. and 7 a.m., right? Well, yes and no. The Internet is a fantastic resource for homework and research. One hour a day could be restricting how well your kids do at school. We know, it makes your head spin.

In general, we recommend covering the following points with your kids in setting an acceptable use policy:

- What are the acceptable hours of usage?

- What are the time limits per day? Is it different for weekdays and weekends?

- What are appropriate websites and activities?

- What is appropriate language?

- Are digital photos allowed to be exchanged? and with whom?

- What are the rules for signing up to online services?

- Are they permitted to download software?

- Are they permitted to download digital music or videos?

- Are they allowed to be online when you are not home?

- Are voice-chat conversations over the Internet permitted?

- Are webcams permitted?

- Are they permitted to use the Internet outside of the house, such as at a friend's house?

VERY IMPORTANT: **We recommend against webcams for kids unless closely supervised.**

Having a clear list of rules and guidelines between you and your kids will remove any possibility later for claiming they did not know.

Making Kids Aware of Online Dangers

According to *Highlights of the Youth Internet Safety Survey* conducted by the U.S. Department of Justice, "one in five children (10 to 17 years old) receive unwanted sexual solicitations online."

Talk to your kids openly about the dangers of being online, including child predators. If possible, sit down with them and read or watch several news stories available online that include the consequences of falling prey to an online predator. Here are a couple (they may not be still available when you read this book; if not go to Google and search for "child-predators sexual-assault"):

From MSNBC's "To Catch a Predator" television series:

http://www.msnbc.msn.com/id/10912603/

From *America's Most Wanted* television show:

http://www.amw.com/features/feature_story_detail.cfm?id=1053

Make sure your kids understand that the Internet provides anonymity. Just because someone on the other end of a chat or IM window says they are 12 means nothing. They could be anyone, anywhere.

VERY IMPORTANT: **There is a difference between an online chat room and *instant messaging* (or IM). The online chat room is akin to a party line, whereas IM is a one-to-one conversation. Many kids today use IM to stay in touch with friends, which is pretty safe because you can control who is in their contact lists. Chat rooms tend to be open-forum discussions, usually centered around a single topic (such as boy bands or professional wrestling). Educate yourself in the differences so that you do not inadvertently take away something of value to your kids that might not be doing harm.**

As mentioned earlier, illegal downloading of music, videos, games, and so on is another type of danger online. It does not seem like a threat per se, but there are quite a few documented cases where parents have been liable for thousands of dollars in fines or settlements because their children illegally downloaded music from music-sharing sites. Discuss the laws regarding music sharing with kids. Explain the difference between illegal sharing sites and legitimate sites such as iTunes.

From the Recording Industry Association of America (RIAA):

http://www.riaa.com/issues/piracy/online.asp

Avoid Giving Out Personal Information Online

Online child predators have been known to use personal information kids give out online to track them down. They do not need a name and address; sometimes they can deduce who a child is and where he or she goes to school from only pieces of information.

Set guidelines for giving out personal information online and enforce them. Make sure your kids understand what they are and are not allowed to share. Information that needs to be under lock and key includes (but is not limited to) the following:

- Name
- Address, even town
- Photos
- Age or characteristics
- School
- Family names or characteristics
- Friends
- Pets
- E-mail address
- Likes and dislikes
- Any other information that can be used to deduce your child's identity

Make it clear to your kids: When in doubt, leave it out. There is no need to give out personal information online to strangers.

Policing Kids Online

Now that you have done some preparation of your kids, you are ready to turn them loose online and go back to what you were doing, right? Wrong.

Just like you keep an eye on your kids if they are out playing in the yard, you should keep an eye on them while they are sitting at a computer. The next few sections give some useful tips for keeping an eye on them.

Browse in Plain Sight

If kids are doing stuff with computers or online that they know is against the rules, it is just like smoking cigarettes: They are going to do it hidden from you somehow.

Here are a few very simple tips you can do to keep your kids' online habits out in the open:

- Consider placing computers in family common areas instead of locked away in a bedroom.

- If they do have a computer in their bedroom, have a policy that when the computer is on, the bedroom door stays open.

- Drop in at random to spend some time online with them. Ask them to show you around online and to meet their online friends.

- Check e-mail inboxes and sent folders. Ask to see their e-mail address book.

VERY IMPORTANT: **One of the difficulties with monitoring kids is that even looking over their shoulder you may not understand what they are doing or saying. For example, IM users have developed their own lingo made up of abbreviations and acronyms. It is a good idea to educate yourself so you are talking the same language. Here are a few:**

- **F2F—Face to face**

- **NP—Nosy parents (but could also mean no problem)**

- **POS—Parent over shoulder**

- **WTGP—Want to go private? (meaning to a private chat)**

You can find a broader list here:

http://www.missingkids.com/adcouncil/pdf/lingo/onlinelingo.pdf

Monitor and Review Your Kids' Websites and Blogs

Just as important as teaching your kids who they can and cannot talk to online is what they are allowed to post on their website or blog.

Websites used to be at least a little difficult to get set up. However, with the explosion of blogging sites such as MySpace.com, it is exceptionally easy for everyone to have a personal blogging site.

Here are some additional tips dealing with websites and blogs:

- Check out your kids' websites. Ask them to show them to you.

- Google your kids. Run a Google search and see whether all the websites you were told about are the only ones out there.

- Check out their friends' websites.

- Check out your kids' blogging sites (see next section).

- Get to know your kids' online friends just like you would if they came to your house.

- Check the website history in Internet Explorer to see where your kids are spending their time (see "Review Website History" section).

Finally, you may want to have a policy with your kids that you need to review proposed content that will be posted on their website or blog site.

Check Out Your Kids' Blogs

Blogging is all the rage with kids and adults alike. Instead of just a website that stays the same most of the time, blogs are more interactive, allowing both the owner and friends to post to each others' sites. Blogs are kind of like an online get-together or journal.

One of the most popular blogging sites is MySpace.com:

> http://www.myspace.com

MySpace has been in the news a lot lately, and not always for a happy headline. MySpace thoughtfully places a restriction that kids who are 14 or under are not able to have their profiles or blogs browsed by anyone except those people they explicitly invite to be on their friend list.

Sounds good. But kids are routinely lying about their age so that their blogs can be "public."

We recommend taking a look at your kids' profiles and blogs on any blogging sites such as MySpace.com. Figure 6-1 shows how to search for your kids' MySpace site using their e-mail address.

Figure 6-1   Searching for Your Kids on MySpace.com

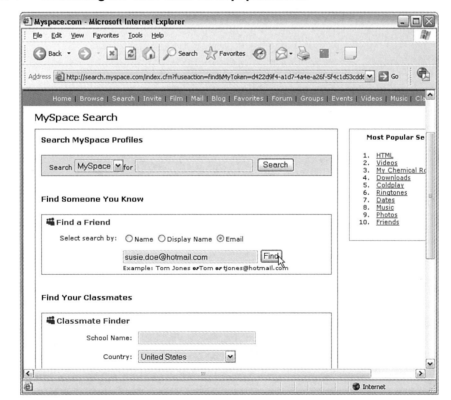

Keep in mind that with free e-mail services, such as Yahoo! Mail and Hotmail, your kids can set up their own e-mail address in about 30 seconds. So, do not assume that just because you do not get a "hit" on the e-mail address you know about that they do not have a blog site. It could be listed under an e-mail address they created themselves without your knowledge.

It also could be the case that your child (assuming they are younger than 14) is following the rules and therefore his or her profile is not visible. In this case, you might need to have them invite you to their friends list so that you can view their material.

When reviewing your kids' blog sites, ask yourself: If you were a child predator, could you learn anything about your children from their blog that would make them vulnerable or trackable?

Review Website History

Another way to check up on your kids' online habits is to review the history list of websites they have visited. To do so, go to their computer, open Internet Explorer, and click the **History** button on the toolbar. Figure 6-2 shows an example.

Figure 6-2   Reviewing Browsing History in Internet Explorer

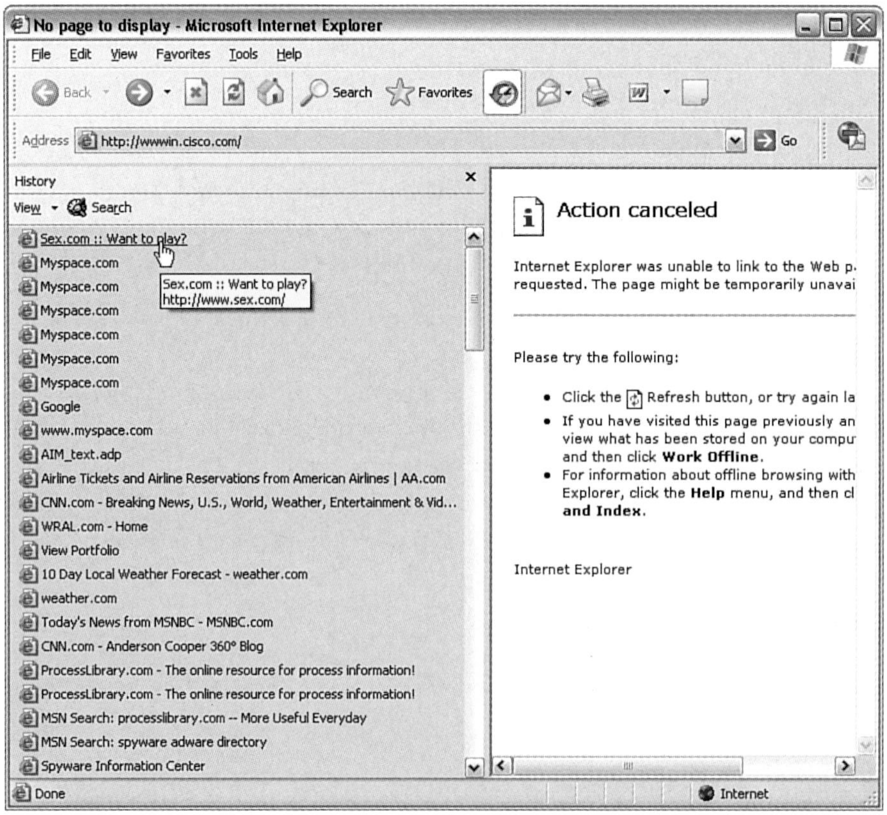

You can see in this example that someone browsed a website within the last day with the URL http://www.sex.com. History is not a reliable option because there are a couple pretty easy workarounds. Smart kids can clear the history or set Internet Explorer not to track history at all. You may want to check the settings under **Tools > Options > General**.

VERY IMPORTANT: **One thing to keep in mind is that in general kids under the age of 12 or so do not visit adult sites on purpose or at least do not go looking for them. If you discovered that your young child has visited one of these sites, it could be an innocent mistake usually from a mistyped website address. In this case, give your child the benefit of doubt unless you see a pattern of looking at these sites emerge.**

A workaround that kids sometimes use is to download an alternative Internet browser and use it instead of Internet Explorer. These include Firefox, Opera, Avant, and Netscape. Check the list of shortcut icons on the desktop and the installed programs list to see whether one is being used.

VERY IMPORTANT: **Windows XP (and other versions of Windows) supports having different login user IDs for a single computer. Each user ID gets its own environment, including a separate set of temporary Internet files and history. So either do not set up login user IDs and everyone can use a common family user ID, or if you do set up a family computer with multiple user IDs, make sure you are logged in to the child's user ID when monitoring and checking things such as Internet browser history.**

Using Parental Controls

Parental controls software allows you to restrict what your kids can and cannot do online, patrolling their computer even when you are not nearby. A number of options can block inappropriate content. The best programs enable you to choose specific types of material to block based on what you think is inappropriate for your child. Some even allow tiers for different age ranges. The various filters are enabled based on the user login (each of your children gets a login ID and password) so that you can have different settings for different age children.

You definitely want to choose a program that has automatic updates from the vendor and one that uses a combination of manually entered URLs and behavior logic to actively scan sites for inappropriate content. Chat recorders are also a good feature to look for, but make sure you get one that records both sides of the chat. Avoid programs that require you to enter all the URLs (addresses) you want to block. You could do nothing but enter porn URLs every minute for the rest of your life and still not catch even half of them.

The first step in enabling parental controls on your home network is to make two decisions:

- What types of controls do you need?

- Where will you put your enforcement point?

Parental controls we can enable include a number of possibilities, not just blocking website access. Most parental control programs include features to do the following:

- Restrict website access by site (in other words, block URLs)

- Restrict website access by content (in other words, scan pages of nonblocked URLs for inappropriate content and then block them if present)

- Restrict which programs can be used (such as web browser, e-mail, chat, IM, music sharing)

- Enforce time limits and hours of usage

Most parental control programs start with a recommended profile for many of these options, based on age group. We recommend starting with those and then make exceptions as situations arise. Second, there are now a number of possibilities for where you put your enforcement point (in other words, where is the traffic cop that controls access). Possible enforcement points are as follows:

- In the ISP network

- In your router

- On each computer in your home network

Each has advantages and disadvantages. For example, it might seem intuitive to only place parental control on a child's computer. However, is it possible they could access your computer and bypass the controls? Still, applying parental controls on every computer in your home network could be cost-prohibitive (depends how many computers you have to protect). It could also be a little cumbersome to make updates to several computers if you need to change access rules.

For these reasons, parental control provided by the router or the ISP might be a better option because it provides a single, central enforcement point; and this is an increasingly popular way to go. If you are really, really concerned, another possibility is to apply parental control in layers (like security), with a central router/ISP-based enforcement point coupled with parental control software on the child's PC.

The sections that follow show how to enable each of these options: ISP-based, router-based, and computer-based parental control.

VERY IMPORTANT: If you take all the precautions, how will you know they are working and have not been circumvented? One way is to periodically log in to the computer (using the child's user ID if you have implemented multiple user IDs) and test the controls. Try doing things that are against your policy, such as browser adult websites and so on. Just make sure your spouse knows so that a child does not get falsely accused due to your test.

Parental Controls at Your ISP

Many service providers offer built-in parental control as part of their service. Check with your service provider to see whether this is an option. Most of the bundled parental services work by installing an Internet browser that is specific to the service (for example, AOL, EarthLink, MSN) and then only using that browser for accessing the Internet.

This type of protection works in preventing the completely inadvertent access into adult content, such as making a typo in a website and your child ends up on a porn site staring at unmentionables on the screen, probably to their horror as much as yours. Just keep in mind, though, that the controls are only as good as the willingness to use their modified Internet browser. Most kids beyond the age of eight can quite easily figure out how to circumvent the controls.

Turning on parental control at your service provider will vary highly and depend entirely on how they have chosen to set up their services. Follow these steps to set up your services (we use EarthLink here as an example):

Step 1   Log in to your ISP account. Under Profile Management, find the Parental Control setting for the child's account. Set it to **On**.

Step 2   Click **Profile Settings**. With this particular service, you can specify the child's age, and the access controls are set accordingly (see Figure 6-3). Click **Save**.

Figure 6-3   Example of EarthLink's Parental Control

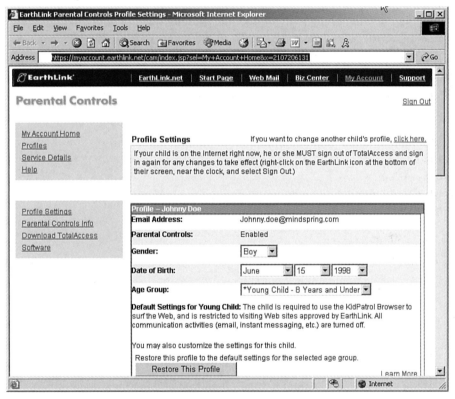

Step 3   Click **Web Browsing Settings** (see Figure 6-4). The options have been set appropriately to the child's age (eight, for our example):

- Must use KidPatrol browser

- Mask all inappropriate website content

- Allow access to approved websites only

Step 4   Click **Save**.

Figure 6-4   **Setting Your Child's Profile**

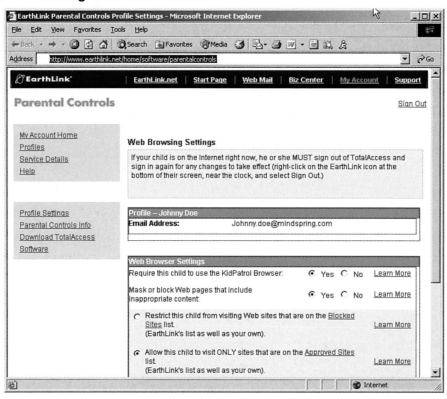

To take advantage of the parental controls with this service, everyone must use the specially provided EarthLink TotalAccess browser with integrated security functions. Then each family user must log in with his or her user ID and password. Access privileges are set according to each person.

Again, this type of protection is adequate against inadvertent access to adult content, but probably not that difficult to circumvent. For example, someone wanting to access adult material might be able to download a different browser.

VERY IMPORTANT: **Another possible circumvention is to connect to the Internet through a neighbor's nearby unsecured wireless connection. You might want to periodically check the list of wireless networks that are in the preferred list on your child's computer. On Windows XP, you can go to Start > Control Panel > Network Connections, select the wireless connection, click Properties, and check the Wireless Networks tab.**

Parental Controls at Your Home Network Router

Another (more recent) option is to use your home network router as the parental control enforcement point. Linksys has partnered with Netopia to offer a service where the Linksys router works in conjunction with a centralized service to provide parental control. The service requires an annual subscription for $40 ($3.33 per month seems like a bargain to us!).

The model is similar to the ISP model, in that each user logs in with a user ID when accessing the Internet. Based on the account, privileges are enforced by the router. A major advantage of this approach is that the enforcement is provided for your entire home network, regardless of the computer used to access the Internet. Another major advantage of this approach is that it is not dependent on the web browser being used; enforcement occurs regardless.

If you want to go with this type of parental control, you need to make sure the wireless router you buy supports the feature. At the time the book was written, the WRT54GS—Wireless-G SpeedBooster Router model was the first to support the feature.

Follow these steps to set up parental control (on Linksys WRT54GS):

Step 1 Access the wireless router using a web browser. Click **Access Restrictions > Parental Control** (see Figure 6-5).

Click **Enable** to activate the feature on the router.

If you have not done so already, click on **Sign up for Parental Control service** to create a service account.

Click **Save Settings**.

Figure 6-5   Enable Linksys Parental Control

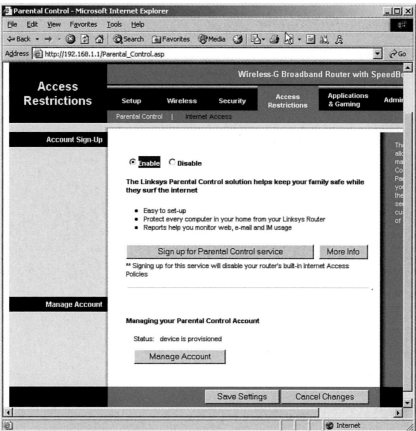

Step 2 Click **Manage Account**.

Click **Family Settings > New Family Member** (see Figure 6-6).

Create an account for each person in your family who will use the Internet, specifying their age. Write down the account user IDs and passwords.

Click **I'm Done**.

Figure 6-6 **Setting Up Family User IDs and Profiles**

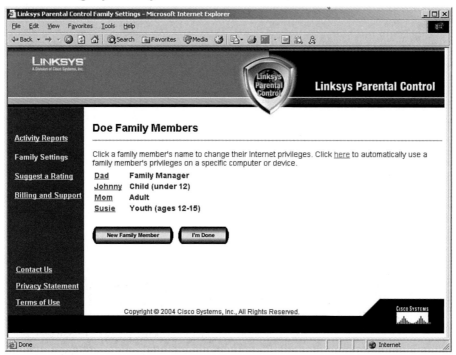

Step 3 Click the child's new user ID (Susie in our example) to change her usage settings.

Click the appropriate areas to change settings, including access times, web restrictions, and e-mail and IM restrictions (see Figure 6-7).

Click **Save**.

Now whenever someone in your house attempts to access the Internet, the router is going to prompt for his or her user ID and password (see Figure 6-8).

Figure 6-7   Modifying User Privileges and Settings

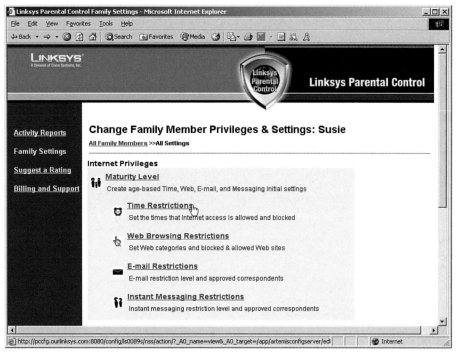

Figure 6-8   Log In to Obtain Internet Access

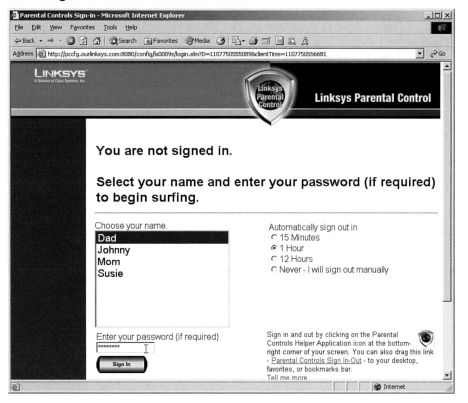

Because the enforcement point is the router, not a computer, it is not possible to circumvent the controls by changing computers or downloading a different web browser.

Another fantastic feature of this service is the ability to periodically look at usage logs and reports to do a little proactive monitoring to see whether the rules you have set are doing their job (see Figure 6-9).

Figure 6-9   Checking Activity Reports

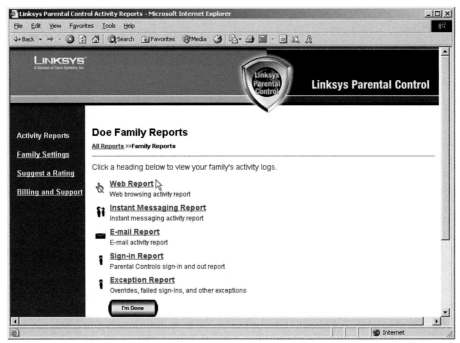

In our opinion, this is the model for the future of parental control. It makes a lot of sense.

VERY IMPORTANT: Again, smart kids can circumvent even router-based parental controls. They could connect to a neighbor's nearby unsecured wireless network. They could also perform a "quick swap" while you are out, possibly connecting their computer directly to the broadband modem and bypassing the router. So be on your toes and check things out.

Parental Controls on Your Computers

Still another possible enforcement point for parental control is to use parental control software on each computer. Parental control software works in a similar model to other software previously discussed, such as antivirus and spam blocking. With the software you purchase, you get an annual subscription that includes periodic downloading of the latest lists of known adult content on the Internet.

Security Bundle Option

Again, the software security bundles discussed in Chapters 1, 3, and 5 ("Tip 1: Use Firewalls," "Tip 3: Use Antivirus Protection," "Tip 5: Lock Out Spyware and Adware," respectively) all support some form of parental controls. The following steps show the process for enabling parental control with the Symantec product. The other security bundles are similar:

Step 1   Double-click the **Norton Internet Security** icon on the desktop. Click **Parental Control**.

Step 2   If it is set to Off (default), click **Turn On** and then **Configure** (see Figure 6-10).

Figure 6-10   Turning On Parental Control in Symantec Norton Internet Security 200x

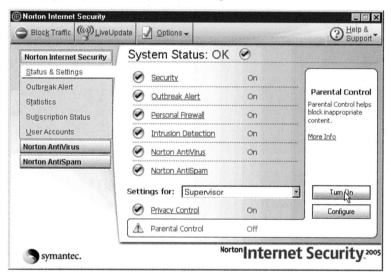

Step 3   With most products, you can set up different profiles for each user of a shared computer.

Select the user you want to set the parental control settings for, and then click **Sites, Programs, Newsgroups,** and **Defaults** to customize the restrictions you want to enforce for each (see Figure 6-11).

Figure 6-11 Customize Restrictions for Each User

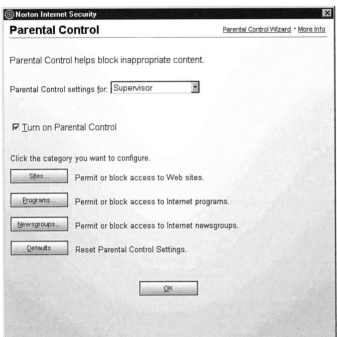

To test the parental controls, launch your Internet browser and enter a URL that is likely to be blocked (http://www.sexsite.com, for example). You should see a rejection like that shown in Figure 6-12.

Figure 6-12 Example of Restricted Website Being Blocked

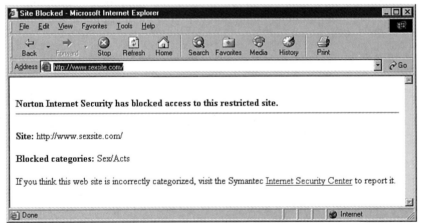

The parental control in the software security product bundles seem to work well. We tested a number of websites hosting adult content, including "gray" area sites that are not all adult material but have some adult material. All in all, the products seem to perform pretty well and as far as we can tell are pretty difficult to circumvent. (Nothing is impossible to circumvent given enough time, energy, and cleverness—and teens are full of all three.)

The disadvantage of this approach is that every computer on your home network must have parental control installed and maintained.

VERY IMPORTANT: **This is a good time to mention the importance of keeping passwords safe. Chapter 8, "Tip 8: Create Strong Passwords," discusses how to use strong passwords. It's also important to keep them safe, meaning if your child (or others) finds out your password or knows where you write it down, then your parental controls are pretty much useless. So, use strong passwords, do write them down, but keep them a secret.**

NetNanny Option

Looking for a much more software-restrictive level of control? You might have a look at other products that are specifically focused on parental controls. There are numerous products. Check parenting magazines and consumer guides for recommendations. One such product that we evaluated is NetNanny, available here:

> http://www.netnanny.com/

NetNanny installation is like any other software installation, so we skip that part and go straight to setting up the rules. There are numerous features and controls in NetNanny; we only scratch the surface. Double-click the **NetNanny** icon on the desktop to bring up the control window. Here, you can set the level of restriction to 1, 2, 3, or 4 for website blocking (see Figure 6-13). Set the level that is appropriate for your family.

Figure 6-13   Setting Level of Restriction in NetNanny

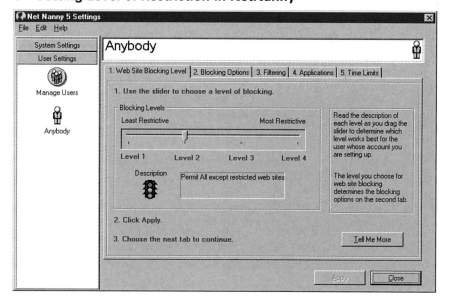

You can then proceed through the different settings to provide your rules for programs that can and cannot be used, whether to scan pages for objectionable content, and so on.

One nice feature to point out is the ability to limit usage to certain days and times, or provide a daily limit to time spent on the Internet (see Figure 6-14). No more 2 a.m. IM sessions!

Figure 6-14   Setting Internet Access Time Limits

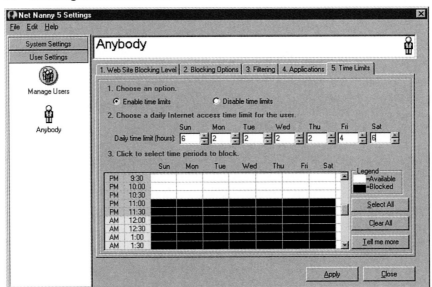

By the way, we installed NetNanny "on top of" Symantec Norton Internet Security 200x and the two worked together. The parental control provided by the Symantec product caught a lot of attempts to access what were clearly adult content sites. NetNanny tended to be more restrictive, jumping in where Symantec left off.

What to Do If You Think Your Child Is Abusing the Rules

Most of the tips we provide in this section are well known, but some of these solutions can be considered an invasion of privacy because the child (or spouse) will not be able to detect the monitoring tools used. It is always best to be upfront with your children (and spouse); when someone is knowingly violating household rules, however, we believe that it is your right to take action.

Activity Loggers

If you reach the point where you believe a child is not playing by your rules (for example, you think they may have dark circles under their eyes from instant messaging with their friends at 2 a.m. each night) and you have exhausted all other measures, it is probably time to try some Internet activity tracking and logging.

They work like a VCR for your computer screen and can be played back later. The best ones operate in "stealth mode," meaning their operation is nearly impossible to detect even by savvy computer users. Some programs even send screen captures to a website that allow you to view the screen remotely. These programs are a bit more expensive than the typical filter programs mentioned and are usually used as a last resort.

Here are a couple of Internet-tracking programs that are recommended by various computer magazines:

- **Activity Logger**—http://www.softactivity.com/

- **AceSpy**—http://www.acespy.com

- **Spector**—http://www.spectorsoft.com/

VERY IMPORTANT: **These programs can also be useful for monitoring spouses who may be doing some stuff online that is ... how should we put it ... not exactly conducive to the marriage. Now, the authors are not marriage counselors, and if a spouse will seek out these venues on the Internet, chances are there are serious problems in the relationship anyway. As the saying goes: Where there is a will, there is a way. But, this section would not be complete without mentioning that the same Internet activity logger tools that can be used to track what a child is doing on the Internet are also just as useful for tracking spouses. Enough said.**

Each monitoring program is different, and we obviously cannot cover them all here. So, we chose one named Activity Logger because the name is easy to remember, and they had a free trial download. The installation of Activity Logger is straightforward, and so in the interest of space, we skip it. However, it is worth pointing out that during installation several options are presented related to how "hidden" the program is in the computer. Hidden is good. In general, you want to follow these guidelines:

- *Do not* create any icons for the logger. If a new icon appears on the desktop or the Windows toolbar, you are busted.

- *Do not* have the running program show up on the Windows toolbar as a running task.

- *Do not* have the program show up under the Add/Remove Programs function in Windows.

- *Do* have the program start when Windows starts. You want the program to always be running when the computer is being used.

You can set the logging options you want by accessing the program's setup function (because it is hidden, you probably have to launch this directly from the installation directory on the hard disk). Set up whatever logging options you want (see Figure 6-15). Set the log file size to be large enough for how much usage time you want to capture.

Figure 6-15   Configure Your Logging Engine

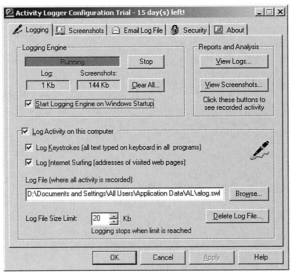

Now that you have the program set up to log and hidden, time to sit back and let it do its magic. After some period of time (overnight or whatever makes sense), you can go view the logs. Figure 6-16 shows a sample Activity Logger log.

Figure 6-16   Sample Log from Activity Logger

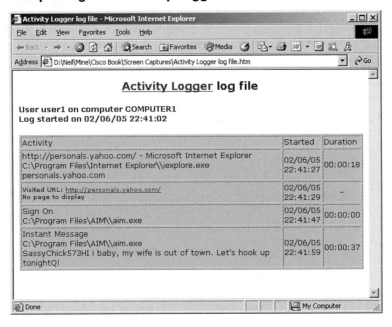

VERY IMPORTANT: Remember that logging of this nature captures everything done on the computer, good and bad. There may be lots and lots of good to wade through to see any bad. Lots of data will be logged. So, do not take logging lightly. If you really need to go to this level of monitoring, prepare yourself for some time needed to wade through lengthy logs.

From Figure 6-16, we can tell that someone used the computer around 10:21 p.m. First, they used Internet Explorer to go to Yahoo! Personals. Next, they started an AOL IM session to someone with an IM nickname of SassyChick573. So, right there we know something is up.

Here's another pretty cool feature of Activity Logger (and other programs have it as well): It can take full-screen snapshots at intervals so that you can see exactly what was being displayed on the computer screen while the person was using it. Figure 6-17 shows a sample of a tracked session.

Figure 6-17   Sample Screen Shot of a Tracked Internet Session

Now, we can actually see what the person was doing on Yahoo! Personals. Much harder to claim, "Oh, I just landed on that page by accident" if you have screenshots of the person doing searches and interacting with people. We can also see the actual text being typed on both sides of the IM conversation. In this example, the originator typed, "Hi baby, my wife is out of town tonight. Let's hook up!" Yikes, let's see someone explain that away.

VERY IMPORTANT: **We are pretty sure that using the programs discussed in this chapter is legal when you are monitoring your kids, but not sure what the laws are regarding tracking of spouses. Check the laws in your state. We are not lawyers; trust us, neither of us had the attention span to sit through law school.**

Summary

The Internet is a fantastic place with so much information it can make your head swim. Kids can learn a lot by being online, but there are also dangers they need to be protected from.

There are tools to help parents restrict what their kids do and see on the Internet. But, we stress that no program is a substitute for open communication with your kids. Decide on what the appropriate usage policy is for your family, communicate it openly to your kids, and enforce consequences if they abuse the privilege.

Where to Go for More Information

To learn more about safety for children on the Internet, here are a few websites you can refer to:

http://www.cybertipline.com

http://www.getnetwise.org

http://www.safekids.com/

http://wiredsafety.org/

http://www.microsoft.com/athome/security/children

We seemed to have misplaced your account number...

Bank

CHAPTER 7

Tip 7: Recognize and Avoid Phishing Scams

Threat Type: Victim enabled

Examples of Threats:

- E-mails asking for account information that will then be used by identity thieves

- E-mails "selling" security services

Our Tips:

- Never click any of the links within the e-mail.

- Never send account information via e-mail.

- Never reply to any e-mail asking for personal or account information, even if a phone number is provided.

Phishing is a relatively new social engineering scam that has become one of the most popular tactics used by identity thieves. Phishing scams play on people's fear or sense of doing what is right by tricking victims into willingly supplying scammers with personal information, account numbers, passwords, and mothers' maiden names. Some thieves take it a step further with confidence scams that offer "identity security" to their former victims and then hit them again.

VERY IMPORTANT: **For those unfamiliar with the concept of *social engineering*, Wikipedia.com defines it as the practice of obtaining confidential information by manipulation of legitimate users. A social engineer will commonly use the telephone or Internet to trick people into revealing sensitive information or get them to do something that is against typical policies. By this method, social engineers exploit the natural tendency of a person to trust his or her word, rather than exploiting computer security holes. It is generally agreed upon that users are the weak link in security, and this principle is what makes social engineering possible.**

Your Bank

Your real credit card company is not involved at all, but the scam site and e-mail look legitimate.

1 You receive a fraudulent e-mail posing as your credit card company.

Mr. Anderson: Please click this link to verify your credit card information.

Your Computer

Never respond to an e-mail request for account-number verification. If you really think that your credit card company forgot your account number, go shopping! If you have questions, call the 1-800 number on the back of your card or check your monthly statement.

2 A link to fraudulent imposter's website is provided in the e-mail.

Imposter Web Site

3 You enter your credit card info.

Please enter your credit card number.

Please enter your Social Security number to verify identity.

Thanks!

Thank you, Mr. Anderson. Your credit card information has been verified.

4 The thief now has your credit card to use online.

Credit Card List
5555-4444-3333-2222
5555-4444-3333-1111
5555-4444-3333-0101

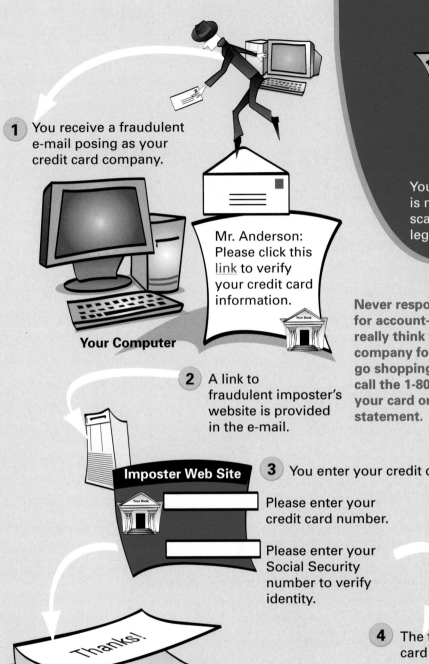

To give you an idea how widespread this problem has become, the following statistics were taken from http://www.mailfrontier.com (with the original source reference included). In 2005

- **5.7 billion** phishing e-mails were sent each month (Anti-Phishing Work Group).

- **$1200** was the average loss to each person successfully phished (Federal Trade Commission).

- **13,228** unique phishing attacks (on average) were launched per month (Anti-Phishing Work Group).

- **3431** phishing websites were created (on average) each month (Anti-Phishing Work Group).

In others words, this is a pretty big problem. If you fall for one of these scams, you could be looking at real financial losses, and potentially years to repair your credit rating. The key realization is that there would not be all this phishing activity going on if people were not falling for it. Figure 7-1 shows a typical sample phishing e-mail (provided by Wikipedia) and demonstrates exactly how legitimate they can appear.

VERY IMPORTANT: **The term *phishing* is kind of a funny spelling of the word *fishing*, referring to fishing you for your identity. The *ph* instead of *f* in the spelling gets its origins from the term *phreaking*, which is a form of hacking into phone lines to get free long distance. There is still some debate on exactly how and when the use of the term got started, but most people assume it is a combination of the words phone and freak. This spelling convention has carried over to computer hackers for hacks such as pharming and phishing.**

Figure 7-1   Phishing Example

TrustedBank™

Dear valued customer of TrustedBank,

We have recieved notice that you have recently attempted to withdraw the following amount from your checking account while in another country: $135.25.

If this information is not correct, someone unknown may have access to your account. As a safety measure, please visit our website via the link below to verify your personal information:

http://www.trustedbank.com/general/custverifyinfo.asp

Once you have done this, our fraud department will work to resolve this discrepency. We are happy you have chosen us to do business with.

Thank you,
TrustedBank

Member FDIC © 2005 TrustedBank, inc.

How Phishing Scams Work

The typical phishing scam begins with an e-mail that looks entirely legitimate. The e-mail can appear to be from a bank, online auction company (such as eBay), money-transfer service (such as PayPal), or even a charity. Often, the e-mail states that your account is about to expire (or will be suspended) unless the person's account information is verified. A link to a website is usually provided. When you click the link, you are directed to a web page that prompts you to enter your account information or passwords or credit cards numbers or some other sensitive (and potentially damaging) information, or all of the above.

The problem is, even though the website you were taken to looks legitimate, the website is a fake whose only purpose is to capture that valuable account and password information, or worse, your credit card information.

Phishing scams can also be sent via instant messaging or even as invites to online contact libraries.

From the perspective of the thieves, this is a good business because they literally send millions and millions of e-mails out using automated programs. Even just a few responses make the effort worthwhile. When they have a mark, they empty the victim's accounts and move on to the next one. These folks are usually set up in countries with no extradition laws, and they move around a lot. So, even if the authorities find them, it is difficult to bring them to justice.

Tricks of the Trade

One reason phishing schemes have become both more prevalent and more successful is the wide availability of powerful publishing and graphics programs that scammers use to create legitimate-looking e-mails, complete with corporate logos and letterheads and graphics. In addition, the scammers create web pages that are nearly indistinguishable from the real corporate sites they are mimicking. Some go so far as to copy the exact navigation structure of the real website so that when you click the link you are taken to a page that looks just like the one that you would find if you typed in the real URL. When you type in your login ID and password, they (the identity thieves) can immediately go to the real site, log in, and gain access to all of your information (and have the ability to do anything you could do on the site in question).

This is all a bit daunting, and although we pledge not to go over the top with scare tactics in this book, this is one scam you should always be on the alert for. Some of these e-mails look amazingly legitimate. If you do not want to take our word for it, go to the following URL, which provides a phishing IQ test:

http://survey.mailfrontier.com/survey/quiztest.html

Good luck guessing which ones are real and which ones are phishing attempts. (Just in case the site gets moved, you can also go to Google or some other search engine and search for "phishing IQ test.")

Be sure to look at the "why" portion of the results; it explains how you can tell whether the e-mails are real.

This does seem pretty scary, but there is some good news; there are usually some specific giveaways within these scam e-mails, and even without the clues there are things you can do to avoid being taken advantage of.

One hard and fast rule is that you should *never, under any circumstances*, click a link from an e-mail that you even remotely suspect as not being legitimate. In fact, even if you do not suspect the e-mail of being a fake, you should still not click the links in the e-mail. The reason for this is that it is a simple matter to redirect a link on a page or in the text of an e-mail to any other site. For example, if I enter **http://www.citibank.com**, you would think that clicking the link will take me to Citibank's corporate website. I can tell this by rolling my cursor over the link in Microsoft Word, which shows a popup window noting where the hyperlink is directed to. Figure 7-2 shows that the hyperlink does in fact link to the appropriate URL.

Figure 7-2   Legitimate Website Hyperlink

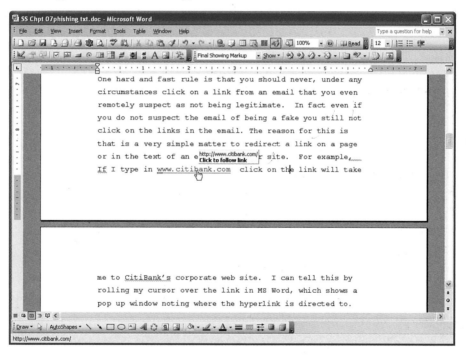

As we said, however, it is very simple thing to change where the link is directed, as demonstrated in Figure 7-3. As you can see, the text still shows that it goes to the corporate site. However, the link will actually send you to a place you probably do not want to go (much less type in your credit card number when there).

Figure 7-3   Phishing Scam Redirect

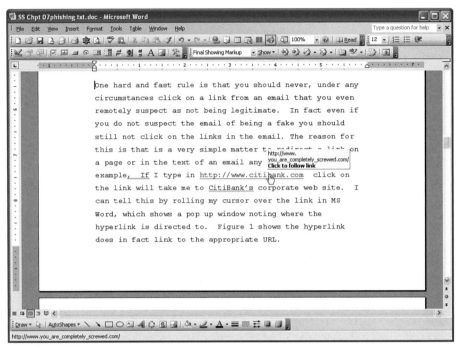

Of course, this is easy to see in Word, but chances are your e-mail client does not have the link rollover feature. Even if it does, chances are you are not paying attention to it. Unless the actual URL that you get directed to does not look like what you expected, you might never even notice that you are not on a legitimate website. In any case, most scammers take care that the site looks legitimate so that you do not bother looking at the address bar in your browser.

If you do need to go to the link in the e-mail for whatever reason, the best thing to do is to manually type in the URL (address) into the address window in your Internet browser. You can also Google the name of the company you are trying to reach and click the link in the results page. Doing this takes an extra step or two, but at least this way you will be sure you are going to the address you entered and not a redirect.

One more thing: In some cases, a legitimate-looking URL is fake, and even if you copy the text into your browser you could still end up in a bad place. For example, consider the following URL:

www.google.com@halcyon.com/account_control

Did you notice anything odd at first pass? It looks legitimate because it starts with www.google.com. If you just take a quick glance, you might not notice that the base URL is not google; it is actually google.com@halcyon.com. In this case, a scammer just registers a domain name that starts with a known site but has some extra stuff tacked on to it. Figure 7-4 is another example with a URL that appears legitimate.

Figure 7-4   Legitimate-Looking URL Trick

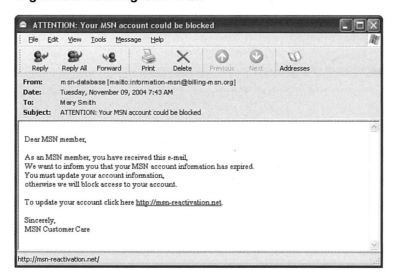

In this case, you might think that you are going to an MSN site; however, if you go to that site and enter your personal information, you are about to get taken.

The lesson here is pay attention and be vigilant. The ".com" is a simple naming convention and not a hard-and-firm rule that governs where a web page actually lives. These extensions include .org, .gov, and .edu, to name a few. You can take any known site, add some other words or letters to the end of it, and register it as a domain name, as long as nobody has already registered the name. You should also be careful about common misspellings and typing errors when manually entering the address. These mis-types will almost always be registered names. In most cases, it will end up being a porn site, but it would not surprise us to see phishing sites set up before long.

How to Avoid Becoming a Victim

The first thing a person can do to help himself/herself is be suspicious of any e-mail stating that an account, or any other information, is needed, even (or especially) when it looks legitimate. The bottom line is that if a company you do business with needs to contact you, someone, somewhere will pick up the phone and call you. (If you are suspicious about the call, call them back using the phone number listed on your bill.) This may not be the case 100 percent of the time, but always be suspicious of these types of e-mails. Healthy paranoia is a good thing. As we have stated in our previous books, if you think your credit card company has really lost or forgotten your account number, go shopping. That is exactly what the identity thieves who sent you the e-mail will do if you "verify" the number via the e-mail. At least this way you can get some new stuff.

VERY IMPORTANT: Some of the scams include a working pay or toll-free number. If you want to call to verify whether an issue exists, do not call the number posted in the e-mail. Use the one in the phone book or on your bill.

For those who do not want to just delete every suspicious e-mail, here are some things to look for:

Do you actually do business or have an account with the company or institution in question? This one would seem like a no-brainer, but there are many known cases of people getting burned by e-mails that should have been deleted as soon as the name or logo appeared on the screen because they should know it does not concern them, legitimate or otherwise. As far as we can reason, people must just feel a sense of obligation to right a perceived error or respond to something that seems authoritative. Don't do it! The scams rely on people doing what they think is the right thing to do. This is how most social engineering scams work. Figure 7-5 shows an example of an e-mail we received. Neither of us bank with this institution.

Figure 7-5   Account Verification E-Mail Phishing Example

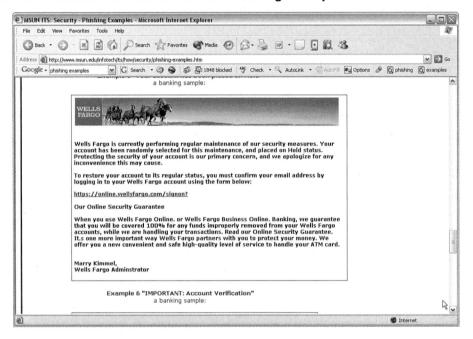

Is the e-mail addressed to a generic title? If the e-mail begins with a greeting such as "Dear account holder" or "Dear *business name* member" or any other greeting that does not use your full name or login ID, it is probably a phishing attempt. Even if it does use your full name or login ID, it might be a scam; if not, however, it should be dismissed outright. In the examples shown (most of the figures in this chapter have generic titles), if the bank knows that all this activity took place on your account, shouldn't they know your name?

Is the e-mail from a strange sender? If the e-mail is from a strange-looking e-mail address (much like spam), ask yourself why your bank does not have a more normal address? If you get an e-mail from MyBank, it is a good bet that the person sending it should have an e-mail address ending in @mybank.com.

Does the e-mail sound urgent, threatening to close an account if you do not take action? The faster you act, the less time you have to think. The people who run these scams want you to move fast so that you give them your personal info before you figure out the scam. Figure 7-6 shows an example of the urgency scam.

Figure 7-6   Urgent Expiration Scam Example

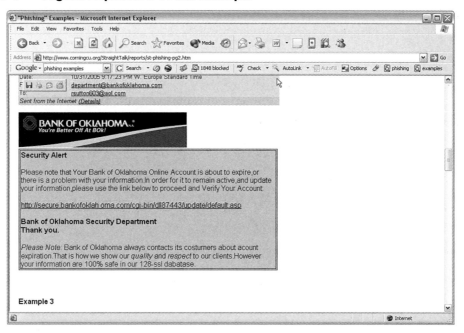

Does the e-mail have misspelled words or poor grammar or sentence structure? Many phishing scams originate overseas or in countries with loose copyright and extradition laws. Although the scammers are talented at creating logos and web pages, they seem to have all skipped language lessons. That is not to say that a perfectly structured e-mail is legitimate. To be sure, however, a poorly written one is a trap.

Does the e-mail ask for charitable donations (often in the wake of a disaster)? The American Red Cross and just about every other reputable charity all have policies in place stating that they do not solicit for donations via e-mail. If you get an e-mail asking for donations, assume it is a scam. If an e-mail alerts you to a relief effort that you want to support, delete the e-mail, open a browser, and go to the official site of the charity you want to support. Do not click any links within the e-mail. This is one of the most insidious forms of phishing, preying on good-intending people and diverting funds from those who would have received additional help. Never respond to an e-mail asking for charitable donations.

Does the e-mail state that you have won a contest or prize that you did not even enter for? It is fake! The previous example showed how scammers prey on people's charity; this type plays on greed. Unless you have specifically entered a contest, do not reply to this type of e-mail. In fact, even if you did enter a contest, do not reply to the e-mail. Call the phone number on the ticket or entry form. Figure 7-7 shows an example of this scam.

Figure 7-7   You Won! Scam Example

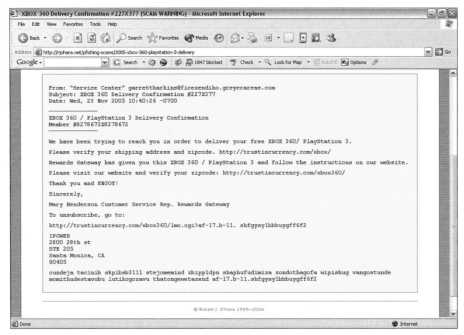

Is the e-mail regarding a transfer of funds from a bank in Nigeria? *Delete Delete Delete*! (also read Chapter 10, "Tip 10: Use Common Sense").

Is the e-mail regarding a recently deceased, wealthy, long-lost relative and you are the only family member they can find? Forward these to your dumb cousin whom you don't like anyway. Really, this has got to be one of the worst scams ever, and yet somehow people fall for it. The e-mail asks for your account information so that they can transfer your inheritance into it. The only transfer that will happen will not be in your favor.

Is the e-mail offering security services through a bank or other type of institution? This is a new version of the confidence schemes. Telemarketers used to do something similar by going back to people they had previously ripped off, offering to track down the stolen money for a fee (thereby ripping them off a second time). In this scheme, people who have been burned, or who are afraid to get burned, are enticed to provide credit card data to pay for bogus services. Figure 7-8 shows an example of this.

These are just some examples of many types of phishing scams out there. The scammers are getting bolder, smarter, and more clever with each scam. So, be on the look out as they are sure to invent new ones every day that do not follow the common examples in this chapter.

Unfortunately, most of the security measures we talk about in this book do not catch or otherwise deter phishing scams (other than spam filters, but those are not 100 percent effective in blocking these types of e-mails). The next section covers what to do if you get an e-mail you suspect as fraudulent. The short answer is if it looks suspicious, delete. You are the best filter.

Figure 7-8   Security Services Scam Example

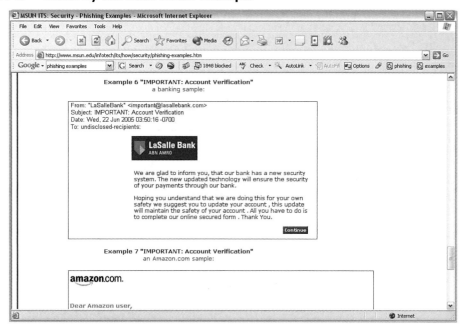

What to Do If You Suspect You Are the Target of a Phishing Scam

The first obvious answer is *do not click the links or reply to the e-mail*! We cannot emphasize this enough. There are basically a couple of things to do after that:

- Notify the actual institution referenced in the scam. Chances are they will already know about it, but you can at least feel like a good citizen for doing your part to help others. After you notify them, delete the e-mail.

- Just delete the e-mail. Chances are the authorities already know about it. Save yourself some hassle.

- If you have already responded to one of these e-mails, call the number on the back of all your credit cards and contact your financial institutions to alert them that you may have been the victim of a scam. You should also check your credit report once a year or so to monitor against suspicious behavior.

- Contact your state's attorney general to report the scam. Also, report the scam to the Federal Trade Commission. The FTC has a website specifically regarding identity theft:

www.consumer.gov/idtheft

Or call 1-877-ID-THEFT.

If for whatever reason you do think you might have an issue with an online account, close the e-mail, enter the URL address you have for the business you deal with, and log in to your account. Better still, call the number on your billing statement and talk to a live person. Never use any of the information provided in the e-mail to contact the party in question.

Summary

Phishing scams are one of the fastest growing and most costly security issues on the Internet, but you can avoid them just by taking the time to look at the request and seeing it for what it is. This type of scam only works when you let it happen. Follow the rules laid out in this chapter and do not be in a rush to respond to official-looking e-mails. Reputable financial and business institutions have largely stopped using e-mail communication and rarely (or never) request personal information via e-mail.

Where to Go for More Information

You can learn more about phishing scams and avoidance methods at the following websites:

http://www.fraudwatchinternational.com/phishing/index.php

http://www.antiphishing.org/

http://www.consumer.gov/idtheft/

CHAPTER 8

Tip 8: Create Strong Passwords

Examples of Threats:

■ When a password is stolen, a thief or hacker can easily access your private information and use your account.

■ Using the "remember password" function on your computer makes you vulnerable, especially if your laptop is stolen.

Our Tips:

■ Create strong passwords that use random combinations of uppercase and lowercase letters, numbers, and characters.

■ Use different passwords for each account.

■ Change your passwords every six months or so.

■ Do not use the remember password function on your Internet browser or other software programs.

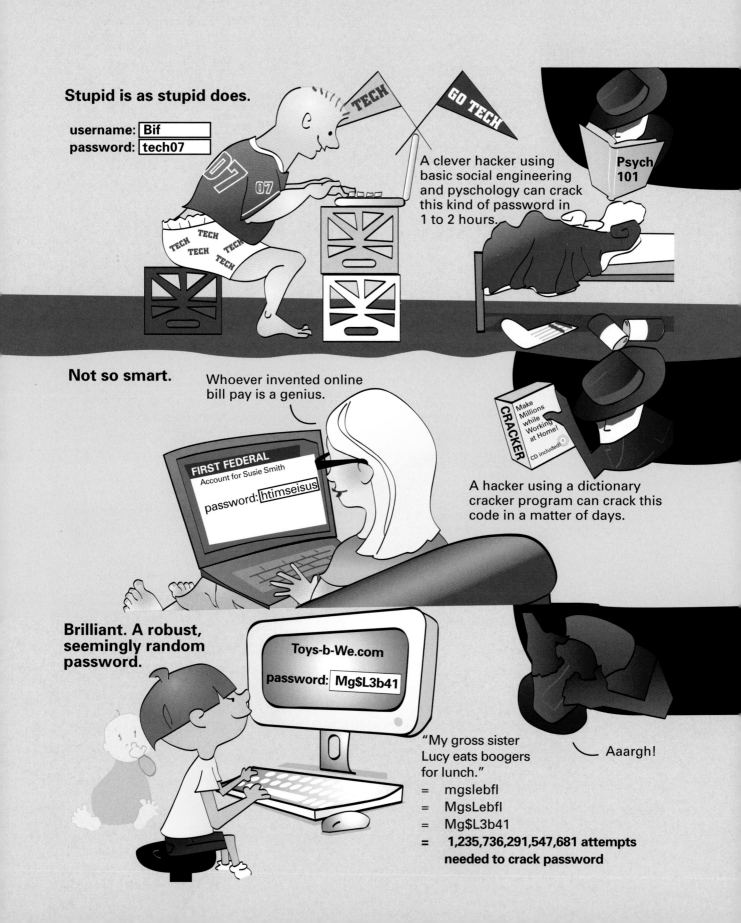

Just about every account you access with your computer requires a password. In fact, you probably have to enter a password just to access your computer. Through the course of a day using your computer, you will likely access several programs or websites requiring a password. If you pay bills online, you will likely have dozens of accounts, each requiring a password. Here are some of the most common applications with password protection:

- Logging in to your computer (Windows login)

- Websites requiring a login account

- E-mail accounts

- Instant messaging services

- Shared network files and directories

- Broadband Internet account

- Administrator access to your home network router

- Wireless network encryption key (for example, WEP or WPA)

Because of the volume of passwords needed, most people create passwords that are easy for them to remember. The problem is that your password is the last line of defense protecting your personal and financial information. Chances are that your passwords are *weak*, meaning they are easy to crack—and we mean really easy. In this chapter, we explain the difference between weak and strong passwords, and we show you how to create strong passwords that are both hard for others to crack and yet easy for you to remember.

Anatomy of a Lousy Password

Before we get started on how to create a hard-to-crack password, let's look at the type of weak passwords that are overused and easy to break. How easy you ask? Well, there is a free and easy-to-obtain program called Crack that can be used to systematically attempt to guess your password, trying out millions of passwords in a matter of hours through the use of an internal dictionary. This dictionary checks against every known word, in just about every language, with all standard manipulations, including character replacements, common misspellings, and letter reorderings. It also checks against names in every language (including the Chinese phone book). If that were not bad enough, it also checks against common character patterns, fictional characters and places, and every real place in the galaxy that has a name. In addition it also checks every date in every format. In other words, if it is a person, a time, an event, a place, a thing, or even a thing's place, or a person's thing, it is a bad idea to use it as a password.

Hackers use programs such as this to conduct what are known as *brute-force password attacks*, meaning they use a program to keep trying password after password until they get a hit. Weak passwords make it much easier for such attacks. Table 8-1 shows some specific examples of weak passwords.

Table 8-1   **Sample Weak Passwords**

Example	What's the Problem
password	This is not clever. Do not use any known words, especially this one.
wordpass	Also not clever and easily cracked because it is made up of common words.
drowssap	Crack (and other programs like it) checks for words written in reverse.
Pa$$word	Crack (and other programs like it) checks for character replacements.
passwurd	Crack (and other programs like it) checks for misspellings, phonetic or otherwise.
Password49	Adding numbers to the end of a word does not make a password harder to crack.
123password	Prefixing words with numbers does not make a password harder to crack.
wachtwoord	Using Dutch (or any other known language, including Klingon and Hobbit) does not help. Crack checks them all.
12345	This is just something an idiot would use on their luggage.
lkjhgf	This is a consecutive string of keyboard characters that is easy to crack.
14159265	Any nonsequential, but algorithmic pattern is easily cracked. (This is the first eight digits of pi to the right of the decimal point.)
abbcccdddd	Any repeating pattern is easily cracked.
mrsmee	Crack (and other programs like it) checks for literary characters.
lordnelson	Crack (and other programs like it) checks for real people and historical figures.
1600pennave	Do not use real addresses. Crack (and other programs like it) checks for them.
22 BakerSt	Crack (and other programs like it) checks for fake addresses, too.
Raleigh	Do not use real places. Crack (and other programs like it) checks for them.
munchkinland	Crack (and other programs like it) checks for made up places, too.
	No password. Although this may be convenient for Windows login, it is ill advised.

These are just a few examples of weak and easily cracked passwords. In general, if you use something familiar to you, Crack and other programs like it will figure it out. Also, you should never use personal information such as dates, login names, Social Security numbers, or any other number associated with you for your password.

Now that we have probably convinced you to change all your passwords, let's look at what it takes for a password to be considered strong.

Elements of a Strong Password

In a few words, a strong password is a random bunch of letters, numbers, and characters, usually eight or more digits long. The eight-character thing is really about the math and not a hard-and-fast rule. In fact, the more digits, the better, but only if the password is truly random. Let's look briefly at why random passwords are so hard for Crack to break.

Assume for a moment that you have a completely random password, one that cannot be found in even the most complete cracking dictionary on Earth. In this case, the only way to crack the password is the brute-force method of checking against all possible character combinations. The best defense against this method is to stack the odds in your favor so that it comes close to mathematically impossible to guess the password.

Here is how that is done. To start with, we have a lot of characters to work with:

- There are 26 letters in the English alphabet (a–z).

- All can be capitalized (A–Z) or lowercase (a–z).

- There are 10 numeric digits (0–9).

- There are roughly 30 other special characters on a standard keyboard (!, <, @, >, ?, and so on). Not all are accepted by password-checking tools, so let's say about 15 of the 30 are.

If you create a truly random pattern of letters, numbers, and characters, there are about 77 possibilities for each digit in the password. If you use 8 characters, you raise that number to the power of 8, which gives you 1,235,736,291,547,681 combinations. It would take an awful lot of computing power (and several years) to try all the combinations that would eventually result in the right answer. To make it even harder on any would-be crackers, in addition to using a strong password you should change passwords periodically (we discuss how often a little later).

How to Create a Strong Password That You Can Remember

So here you are, knowing that you need a strong password, but how are you supposed to remember *Dsq#}3frP and 17 other uniquely random passwords for all your various accounts?

The answer is that you can use some personal information that will be easy for you to remember but difficult for others to guess. Here is how:

Step 1   Start with a sentence about you or your family. For example:

My sister Joanne is four years older than my brother Matt.

Step 2   Take the first letter of each word. If you have a number in your sentence use the number. The base password is now:

msji4yotmbm

Step 3   Make case substitutions. With this sentence, we could use the grammatical capitalization for the password, giving us:

MsJi4yotmbM

Step 4   Make character substitutions. Finally, look for opportunities to use other characters that will still be easy to remember, such as $ for *s*. Our final password looks like this:

"M$J!4y0tmbM"

This is a very strong password, nearly impossible to guess, but relatively easy for you to remember.

Additional Password Tips

Here are some additional tips and considerations for passwords:

- **Do not reuse passwords**. If at all possible, try to use a unique password for each of your accounts. If you only have one or two password-protected accounts, this should not be too hard. If you have several, however, it might be difficult to remember them all, even with the technique covered earlier. Consider writing them down in a safe place (but see the next tip).

- **Do not write your passwords down** *unless you can keep them safe*. Most password advice says that you should never write down a password. We think this is a good guideline, but quite frankly most of us have 20 or more accounts. It is better to have a unique password for each account and to write them down somewhere, rather than creating a single password that you use on all your accounts. Here's the trick though: *If you write down your passwords, keep them secured in a locked cabinet or safe*. In your desk drawer or taped under your keyboard are all bad places for a written list of passwords. In a wallet, purse, or backpack is even worse. There are also programs such as Password Corral that allow you to store all of your passwords in a password-protected file on your PC. This way you only need to commit one password to memory. You can also write down the sentence if you used the method in the example earlier (My sister Joanne …); just remember your conversion rules and you can easily re-obtain your password.

- **Avoid using your passwords on public computers**. Even if the remember-password function is turned off, there could be a keystroke logger or other hacking tool that someone has installed. Anything you type could be collected and used against you.

- **Never enable the remember-password option in Windows or Internet browsers**. Even if you are using a computer that no one else uses, do not use this option. (This should be doubly obvious if you are using a shared computer.) Having this option turned on may be convenient, but if you ever lose your laptop (or if it is stolen), someone can easily check all the sites recently visited with your browser and get easy access to all your private information.

- **Never share your password with anyone**. If you do, change it right away.

- **Never send your password in an e-mail**. This is especially the case if you receive an e-mail asking for your account information even if the e-mail looks legitimate. (See Chapter 7, "Tip 7: Recognize and Avoid Phishing Scams.")

- **Change your password periodically**. Some experts advocate changing your passwords every three months. For most accounts, this is a bit much, especially if you create strong passwords such as the one shown earlier. A more realistic period is every six months or so. *Never* go more than a year with any password, and just so you know, rotating passwords among different accounts does not count as changing a password. Use the technique presented earlier and start from scratch. If you think you have been hacked, change all your passwords immediately.

Summary

Most people do not take their passwords seriously enough, opting for something convenient rather than actually protecting their personal information. Do not make this mistake. A good password is your first and sometimes only defense against hackers and identity thieves. You should not use your spouse's name (or any other weak password) no more than you should attempt to lock a safe full of your valuables using a bread tie. Neither of these will stop someone from getting in and taking your stuff.

Where to Go for More Information

Multiple sites on the Internet reference passwords and techniques for how to create them. With the Internet being what it is, it is difficult to determine the original source of the information, but we would like to credit two sites in particular that this chapter is based on.

From Microsoft:

http://www.microsoft.com/athome/security/privacy/password.mspx

By Ryo Furue:

http://iprc.soest.hawaii.edu/~furue/safepass3e.html

In addition, some other great sites can both generate passwords and check passwords for how strong they are.

You can find a good password generator here:

https://www.grc.com/passwords

And you can check the strength of all your passwords here:

http://www.microsoft.com/athome/security/privacy/password_checker.mspx

CHAPTER 9

Tip 9: Back Up Your Files

Threat Type: Software based, victim enabled

Examples of Threats:

- A computer virus destroying or corrupting several of your files

- Failure of your computer hard drive

- Inadvertently deleting a file or folder

Our Tips:

- Back up the data on your computer periodically.

- Store files in your computer under a common file folder (with subfolders, of course) to make it easy to identify your information from the operating system and program files.

Backing up your files is not so much a security measure as it is a good policy against losing important files in the event that you are the victim of a virus or other security breech. It allows you to restore files and bring your computer back to a "previrus" state should you get infected and be unable to remove the virus via a security program. It also keeps you from jumping off a cliff should you be the victim of a hard drive crash that renders all your files inaccessible or destroyed.

Until recently, backing up your system was a complicated and sometimes expensive proposition. Today, storage is inexpensive, and automated back up methods make it easy to do. Still, most people (at least the ones not yet burned by a hard drive crash) simply do not bother with it.

Losing critical (or irreplaceable) files is a painful way to learn about the importance and ease of backing up your files. Storage is cheap, and backing up is easy. This is no different from getting screened for a disease that runs in your family. Early prevention is much cheaper and less painful than trying to fix the situation after you are afflicted.

When considering a plan for file or system backup, three questions need to be answered: what to back up, where to back up to, and how often to back up. These questions are answered in the rest of this chapter.

What Should I Back Up?

There are many, many files on your computer. Which should be backed up? Files can be grouped into three basic types of data files, or tiers: critical files, user files, and system files/programs. Let's take a look at each:

- **Critical files**—These are the files that you simply cannot lose. It could be your list of clients, the transcript of your memoirs, digital photos, key work files, or whatever—any files that would cause you financial ruin, great heartache, or years of work if they were suddenly and irrevocably gone. In most cases, critical files would be those that are updated from time to time, perhaps the exception being photos or other files saved for posterity.

- **User files**—This class of files includes all the files created on your computer or via another program. This includes documents, presentations, e-mails, spreadsheets, and so on. Any file on your computer today that was not there the day you bought it (outside of program files) falls into this category.

VERY IMPORTANT: **In many cases, a critical file can also be defined as a user file. The distinction is really up to you. For example, a person could have two documents, each with a recipe. One recipe came from FoodTV.com, and the other is the only documented recipe of your grandmother's award-winning rutabaga pie. Clearly, there is a difference in the personal value of these two files, so you should have at least some form of backup for the recipe that cannot be replaced.**

- **System files**—This is pretty much everything else on your computer, including the operating system and programs that have been installed.

So, which should you back up? Well, it depends on how much storage you have at your disposal and how quickly you need to be up and running in the event of a problem.

At a minimum, every person who owns a computer should back up critical files. We have seen lives in ruins because of one or two files (determined to be critical after the fact) that were lost or destroyed. Some examples of key files to back up are as follows:

- Financial records

- Digital photographs

- Downloaded music

- Personal project files

- Your e-mail address book

- Saved e-mails

Given that storage is relatively cheap, you should err on the side of designating many files as critical as opposed to being stingy with the critical designation. We recommend that you back up all critical files and user files. Whereas losing all the noncritical files would not push anyone to the brink, it really is a giant pain in the rear end to replace them all or live without them.

Should you back up the operating system and program files? It depends. Most often, you have the CD for the operating system, and either CDs for all the programs you have installed or they are easily downloadable online. If you cannot afford to be without your computer for a day or so while you restore it from CDs, backing up the system and program files is a smart move.

Instead of selecting the subset of files you really need to back up, a final option is to back up the entire system. This is not for everyone because it takes some time and a lot of storage; if you run a business using your computer or cannot afford to be without your computer for a day, however, you might want to think about this option. The most convenient way to back up an entire system is to make a drive image, which is essentially a compressed copy of every bit on your computer. A drive image will cost you a few dollars, but it might be worth it for the piece of mind it provides.

Where Do I Back Up To?

Where to back up files to really depends on what you decide you need to back up, and in this case "where" includes both the device (as in the thing you put the bits and bytes on) and the location (as in where do you put the thing that you put the bits and bytes on):

- **The device**—For critical files, which for the sake of discussion we assume is a handful of relatively small files (the total is less than 1 GB, for example), you are probably okay with using a memory key (we discuss these and other devices later in this chapter) or an online service. For all the user files or a system image backup, you probably ought to consider a zip drive. Zip drives have storage ranges from a few to hundreds of GB of memory. We walk through a couple of user scenarios later in this chapter. There is also the option of installing a second internal hard drive onto your computer; because this means opening your computer, however, we recommend that you avoid this option (and we're not going to tell you how to do it anyway).

- **The location**—Where you keep your storage media depends on how safe you want or need the data to be. For critical files, you should keep your backed up data in a different physical location than your PC. This prevents a disaster (a house fire or earthquake, for example) from destroying both your PC and your backed-up files (unless, of course, it is a *really big* fire or earthquake, in which case your stored files will not be much of a concern to anyone but future archeologists). There are a couple of backup strategies here: "store-and-port" options, in which you back up and then relocate the storage media; and "online" backup, whereby you upload your files to an Internet server far away from where you are.

How Often Should I Back Up?

How often you back up depends on what you are backing up, where you are backing up to, and how often you make changes to the files you back up. For critical files, it really depends on how often you are making changes to them. User files and system files should usually be backed up weekly. A good rule of thumb is that you never want to lose more than a full week of work re-creating updates to files that were lost. For critical files, you do not want to lose more than a day (assuming that it is a working file which changes often). If you are using an automated backup system, it is easy to set it up for automatic daily backups, which could save you a lot of time and aggravation later.

Storage Method Overview

You have a wide range of storage methods available. The one (or ones) you choose largely depends on how much data you have and how critical your data is. The following sections cover the most common methods and provide some guidance on the right storage method for different situations.

Flash Memory

Flash memory, also called memory sticks or USB keys, are a fast and convenient way to store files and provide some level of back up, usually for critical files. They are also small enough to be carried on a key chain. Flash memories come in a number of styles and sizes, and many of the newer ones can be password protected. Some are even designed to withstand extreme physical stress and still maintain their functionality. One of the new trends in Flash memory is biometric security. Access to these memory devices can only be gained by swiping your finger print over the reader. Security measures on such devices is great for secure or private data, but do not forget your password (or lose your finger) because without it the data will be unretrievable. If you do store critical or private information on one of these keys, we suggest spending the extra money to get one with some level of security in case you lose it somewhere.

The available memory on Flash drives is growing, and some Flash drives have up to 32 GB of storage. These are great devices for storing critical files, especially ones that need to be transported. You can also keep these drives in a fire box or safe-deposit box or some other location so that the same disaster does not destroy your computer and backup device. If you do so, be sure to plug the Flash drive into a USB port on a computer once in a while (we are talking once every four to six months, not every week) to ensure the tiny battery inside the Flash device maintains a charge and to make sure the files are still operable (a spot check of one or two files is sufficient). The internal batteries typically last a long time without charging (recharging is automatic when you plug them into your USB port), but read the manual just so you know how long your Flash drive can go without a connection. Backing up to a Flash drive must be done manually, but it is just a matter of copying files from where they are to the Flash drive folder. Figure 9-1 shows where the Flash drive goes.

Figure 9-1   Flash Memory Devices Usually Plug into a USB Port

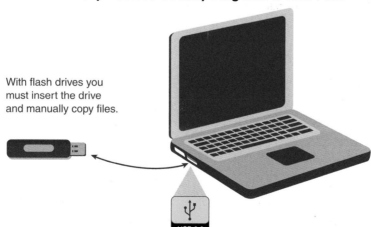

With flash drives you must insert the drive and manually copy files.

We mentioned earlier that it is a good idea to keep all your critical files in a common folder. This makes backing up much faster and easier. Just create a folder called "important stuff" (or whatever works for you) somewhere on your computer. After you have created this folder, move all the folders and files that you have designated as critical to that folder. Now, when you back up, you only need to copy the "important stuff" folder onto the memory key.

There are a lot of choices for consumers here and a wide array of choices regarding size, shape, security, color, and so on. A great resource for sorting all of this out is http://www.cnet.com, where you can read through their ratings on Flash drives and every product type mentioned here (and a bunch that are not). It is a good idea to check here before buying tech gear.

External Hard Drives

External hard drives or zip drives are also great solutions for backing up your files. The capacity of these devices range from tens to hundreds of GBs. You can use them for backing up a few files, all files on a PC, or even for backing up all files on multiple PCs. These drives can also serve double duty by storing massive amounts of digital media, such as digital photos, music, and video libraries on a network.

There are a number of different ways to use external drives, but for backups the best drive on the market is the Maxtor OneTouch (most of the products similar to the OneTouch are good, too). After the initial setup of this device, you literally touch one button on the device to back up your system. There are other options, too, for automated backup in both Windows XP and Windows 98, both of which are shown later in this chapter.

Many of these devices come with both USB and Firewire connections. If your PC has a Firewire port, you will want to use that because the access speed to the storage device is much faster over Firewire than USB.

The downside to these devices is that to have an automated backup process (which is always preferred because you will forget to do it manually), you need to have the device dedicated to a single PC. If you only have one PC that needs backing up, this is no problem; if you have a multi-PC home, however, you must manually move the device from PC to PC to back them up, or buy one external drive per PC, which could get expensive. Figure 9-2 demonstrates how these drives are attached.

Figure 9-2   External Drives Can Plug into a USB or Firewire Port

External hard drives connect directly to your computer's USB or Firewire port. It's easy to set up automated backup schedules.

Networked Storage

One solution to the problem of having multiple computers to back up is to set up a network storage drive. These drives work just like an external hard drive, except that they are connected to your home network device (a wired or wireless router/switch) and can therefore be accessed by all PCs on the network. This is a great setup because you can set up an automated backup routine on all your PCs so that once a week (or at any interval you like) they perform a backup function to the network drive.

With the larger-capacity network storage drives, you can also use the drives as file servers so that all the PCs on the network can access shared digital media libraries, such as digital photos, music, and videos.

Finally, some of the network storage devices can also double as print servers. Figure 9-3 show how these devices connect into your home network.

Figure 9-3   Network Storage Devices Plug into Your Home Network Router

Networked storage devices connect directly to a port on your wired or wireless router. You can set up automated back up routines in Windows XP for each PC. The device can also function as a file server, including for digital media.

Two recommended options for network storage devices are the Linksys attached storage devices and the Buffalo LinkStation drive. If you want to use an existing hard drive, you can also use a network storage link that converts a standard storage device to a network attached storage.

VERY IMPORTANT: **If you do choose the network storage option, your network performance will be noticeably slower during system backups. To avoid any annoying slowdowns, be sure to schedule your backups when the network is not otherwise being used.**

VERY IMPORTANT: **The Linksys NSLU2 is a nice device for converting a standard USB storage device to a network device, but it does require a full reformatting of the storage device. So, if you have data on the drive you want to keep, you need to temporarily store the data on a PC or another hard drive during the reformatting; otherwise, all your data on the device will be lost. This is a cool device, though, because you can take a USB key or external hard drive and then plug the NSLU2 device to your router and your network-based storage. The device is also expandable, so you can connect more than one external hard drive.**

Online Storage

One of the newest options for storage is online storage. Online storage involves you backing up your data over your broadband connection, over the Internet, to a remote company that has many, many file servers (big computers with big storage drives). With these services, your data is stored in several data centers providing backup and geographic separation of all you back up. This is equivalent to what large companies do today for their critical corporate data. Figure 9-4 shows an example.

Figure 9-4   Online Storage Provides Backups in a Remote Location

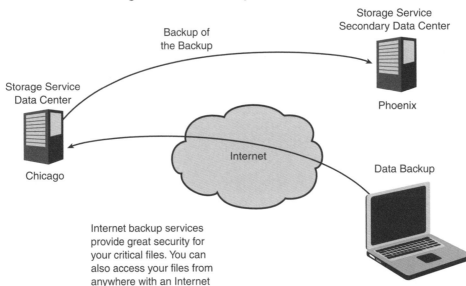

VERY IMPORTANT: **This should be obvious, but do not use this option if you are on a dialup connection.**

A number of companies offer this service. One service, Spare Backup, in addition to all the benefits of the other services, offers a user-friendly introduction and does not require a credit card for the free trial until you actually sign up. Very nice:

> http://www.sparebackup.com

This site also has a feature that assesses what on your PC should be backed up, and they make it pretty easy to customize your backup routine. Figures 9-5, 9-6, and 9-7 provide screen shots of the setup where you select which files to back up.

Figure 9-5   Spare's Automated Backup Assessment

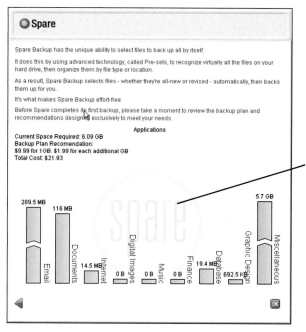

Figure 9-6   Fine-Tuning Which Categories of Files to Back Up

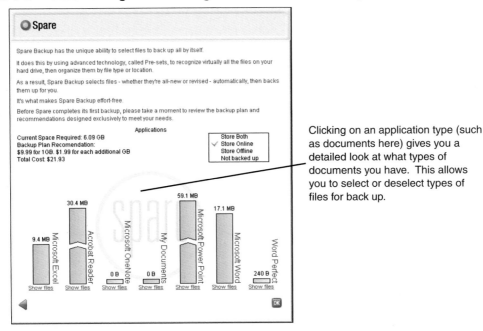

Clicking on an application type (such as documents here) gives you a detailed look at what types of documents you have. This allows you to select or deselect types of files for back up.

Figure 9-7   Fine-Tuning Which Individual Files You Want to Back Up

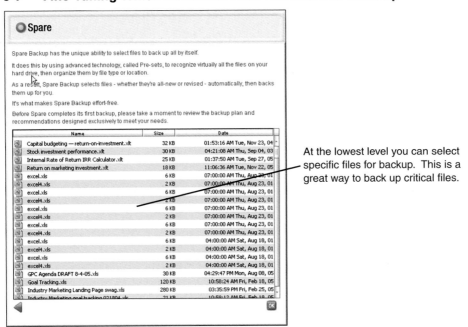

At the lowest level you can select specific files for backup. This is a great way to back up critical files.

Pricing for this service is about the same as other services (the annual fee for 1 GB is about $95), but with this service you can add 1 GB at a time to meet your specific backup needs. Most other services only have predefined tiers (so you pay for storage you do not use). The cost per additional GB per month is less than $2 if you sign up for the annual service.

There are also a number of other services to choose from, including the following:

http://www.ibackup.com

http://www.xdrive.com

http://www.iomega.com/istorage

http://www.backup.com

Most of these sites also offer free trials of 30 days or so, which makes it easy to try them and pick the one that is right for you.

When it comes to online storage and backup, there are three strong advantages:

- Online storage is portable, and you can get easy access to your key files without lugging a lot of gear around with you.

- You are automatically protected from disasters that affect both your PC and your locally backed-up files.

- You can easily set up regularly scheduled backups so that you do not need to remember to back up your files after the initial setup.

On the downside, online storage is relatively expensive compared to other forms of storage, ranging up to hundreds of dollars a year per GB, compared to just under $1 per GB for the external hard drives discussed earlier.

Weigh the critical nature of your files and the convenience you require.

We have found that the online backup services are (in general) secure and provide a good value for truly critical files. If you have data or files that absolutely, positively cannot be lost, an online storage option (in addition to other forms of backup) is the way to go. If you want some additional assurance on your other critical files, online backup services are also a good way to go if you do not mind spending the extra money for the added piece of mind.

DVD or CD Storage

The final alternative here is to back up your files to DVDs (or CDs) using a writable DVD (or CD) system. There are some advantages, including the ability to use the DVD system to both back up and to play music and movies. You can also store key files on disc and store them in a safe place without ever having to worry about shelf life (you will likely expire before the data does as long as you store the disks properly). Figure 9-8 show how a DVD-R drive connects.

Figure 9-8   DVD or CD Drives Can Be Internal or External to the Computer

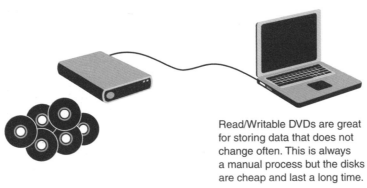

Read/Writable DVDs are great
for storing data that does not
change often. This is always
a manual process but the disks
are cheap and last a long time.

Your computer most likely already has either a DVD or CD drive (check if it is writeable though). To use this method, either the computer manufacturer or DVD drive vendor supplies a software program that can be used to perform backups. It is a manual process, in which you need to decide and select which files to back up (and sit down and perform the backup periodically). But, the discs and drives are cheap, and this is a pretty common type of backup.

There is a way to run backup routines from multiple folders or even multiple computers onto CDs, but we do *not* think this is a good option for most people. It is much easier to move the files to a central folder and then back up that one folder.

Summary of Storage Options

Table 9-1 provides a summary of all the options for backup and storage.

Table 9-1   Storage Summary Table

Storage/ Backup Type	Best Used For	Advantages	Disadvantages	Cost/GB
Flash drive	A few critical files	Flash drives are quick and easy to use and are portable. Memory on these devices is as high as 32 GB at publication time. Everyone should have one of these.	Backup cannot be automated and memory is limited (although increasing every day). Newer devices provide security but most have no security at all.	$50-$100/GB
External hard drive	Backing up user files on a regular basis	Provides massive amounts of storage, and backup routines can be automated.	Because they are co-located with the PC, any disaster that destroys your PC will destroy your backup, too.	~$1/GB

Table 9-1   Storage Summary Table   *continued*

Storage/ Backup Type	Best Used For	Advantages	Disadvantages	Cost/GB
Network storage/backup	Backing up users files from several PCs	All the advantages of an external hard drive plus the ability to back up more than one PC with the same device.	Network storage devices are a bit more complex to set up than external hard drives.	~$1.50/GB
Online storage/backup	Backing up critical files	Probably the safest way to store your data and closest a home user will get to corporate-level backup without spending a ton of money.	The only downside to this type of backup is the cost. It is a great way to back up your files, but you have to pay more for it.	$75-$150/GB per year
DVD-R	Backing up large amounts of data that does not change often (such as music files)	DVD-Rs are a relatively inexpensive form of backup. Once backed up, the disks can be stored just about anywhere and retrieved only when needed.	DVD-R backup cannot really be automated. This is not a good option for backing up files that are updated frequently.	Writers cost between $70-$150. Discs are cheap.

Putting It All Together

In this section, we walk through a possible scenario for two different users to give you an idea or two on which methods would work best for you. Let's take a look at two user profiles:

- **User 1 profile**—User 1 is a college student. He wants to back up his files about once per week. He has several gigabytes of music files that he has purchased over the years, most of which are stored on an external hard drive today. User 1 uses his PC mostly to work on his Master's thesis, which if lost, would basically end his life. This user wants to safely back up his music and store it all away from his apartment. He also wants to keep his thesis work backed up (which is updated often). Because he has an external hard drive, he also wants to back up his user files.

- **User 2 Profile**—User 2 is a homeowner with a spouse and a teenager. All three people in the house have a dedicated PC, and she wants to back them all up onto a single device. She also has about 1 GB of critical files that she wants to keep backed up and very secure.

First let's look at User 1. Given that User 1 already has an external hard drive, he decides to back up his user files directly to this hard drive. If his PC gets infected with a virus, his files can all be recovered. In addition to backing up his PC files this way, he decides to borrow a friends DVD-R writer, and he stores all his music files on DVDs, which he keeps in a box in the trunk of his car. This way, if his apartment burns down, he still has all his music (which for a college kid is pretty important).

Finally, because his degree and possibly his financial future depends on his thesis, he decides to back up these files on his external hard drive, but he also keeps an updated copy on a Flash drive, which he keeps attached to his keychain. The Flash drive is both password protected and has a fingerprint ID so that if he loses the Flash drive no one will be able to view or steal his work.

Next let's look at User 2. This user needs to back up more than one PC, so she uses a network-based storage device that plugs directly into the back of her wireless router. A backup routine is set up in Windows XP, and now wherever the PCs in the home happen to be (as long as it is in range of the router), the backup routines will back up everyone's files to the network storage device. This user also has some very important files and to be as certain as possible that no harm will come to them she subscribes to an online backup and storage service. She pays an annual fee of $150, which is expensive, but she has the piece of mind that whatever she backs ups to this service is as safe as a file can be.

Using Windows XP Backup

If you happen to use a device suitable for automated backup, but it does not come with a software program that allows you to set up an automated backup routine, you can easily set it up yourself using Windows XP. The basic steps are outlined as follows (the following procedure is based on Microsoft's website located at http://www.microsoft.com/athome/security/update/howbackup.mspx):

Step 1   Click **Start>All Programs>Accessories>System Tools**, and then click **Backup** to start the wizard.

VERY IMPORTANT: If you are using XP Professional, the backup program should be pre-loaded. If you have XP Home edition and you did not see anything called Backup in Step 1, you will have to install it from your XP CD. Click Perform Additional Tasks>Browse This CD. This will bring up an Explorer window. Click the following folders:

Value Add > MFST > Ntbackup

When you are in this folder, double-click the Ntbackup.msi file, which will install the backup program.

Step 2   Click **Next** to skip past the opening page, choose **Back up files and settings** from the second page, and then click **Next**.

Step 3   Choose which files or folders you want to back up. You are given several choice here. If you want to back up only select files or folders, click the **Let me choose what to back up** button.

Step 4   Choose where you want the data backed up to. This will likely be the name of the device connected to your PC or on the network. You also need to create a name for the backup.

Step 5   Set your schedule. Click the **Advanced** button and then **Next** and you will see a schedule window.

Summary

We realize that backing up files might not be the most exciting thing to think about, but as we stated, memory is inexpensive and backup routines can be easily automated.

Do not make the mistake of waiting for a massive computer crash, hard disk failure, or rogue virus (or even accidental deletion) to learn how easy it is to back up your files (or how painful it is when you lose all your stuff). It is much better to be that smug person who tells the person who just did lose all his files that you back up your stuff and that it is easy.

Where to Go for More Information

If you have any problems with backup procedures, both Microsoft and Apple have good user help pages on their corporate sites. Just go to http://www.microsoft.com or http://www.apple.com (on the Apple site, click the **Support** tab) and search for "backing up files" or whatever else you need help with, and a slew of articles and help files will appear.

CHAPTER 10

Tip 10: Use Common Sense

Threat Type: Victim enabled

Examples of Threats:

- Bank-transfer scams

- Get-rich schemes

- Urban-legend e-mails

Our Tips:

- Be skeptical of any "deals" or money-making opportunities that you are told about online.

- Spend some time researching and verifying information.

You might be surprised to see a chapter in this book on common sense. Some of you might even be a little insulted. Well, as it turns out, in the human species two things are true:

- Common sense and intelligence are not related or connected in any way.

- Common sense ain't all that common.

Imagine for a moment that you open your front door one morning and there is a note taped to the door with the following letter:

Dear Sir or Madam,
It has come to our attention that you have been engaging in criminal activity in your home. Because we are very busy down here at the police station, we would like you to just go ahead and pay the fine for your misdeeds by placing a large amount of cash in the envelope we have included here as a courtesy.

This will save us all a great deal of time.

Please tape the envelope back to your door, and we will be along shortly to collect.

Thanks for your cooperation,
The Police

Okay, now how many of you reading this think you would actually stuff the envelope with cash? We are guessing not one of you would do it. Many of you would throw the letter out with nothing more than a chuckle, assuming it was a prank played on you by some enterprising 12 year olds. Some of you would maybe even call the police to warn them of the scam.

Now for the sad news: If the note came to you via an e-mail, the statistics suggest that at least a few people would bite on this admittedly simple and poorly thought-out scam. If the scam were a bit more sophisticated, even more people would get taken.

The question is why? Why do people who would normally have some healthy skepticism about "too good to be true" deals when they are out in the real world suddenly become gullible when sitting in front of their home computer? That we cannot answer. But, we can at least make you aware of the tendency people have of letting their guard down while on the Internet.

We break this down into a few categories, starting with some mild stuff that is intended more to keep you from looking foolish, and then move on to more serious stuff that we hope will keep you from stuffing that envelope with cash.

Urban Legends

One of the earliest phenomena of widespread e-mail access was the mass e-mailing of stories warning the reader about some great injustice, funny story, or a once-in-a-lifetime opportunity. The e-mails would get forwarded to hundreds of people who would also forward them, and within a day or two the story would race across the world.

Urban legends have always existed, even before e-mail. But, with the ease of communicating to tens or even hundreds of people with the push of a button, these stories really came into their own during the Internet age.

So, what does this have to do with security? Well, it is our contention that peoples' tendency to forward these stories on to everyone in their address book was an early indication that people were more gullible in cyberspace than in the real world. It was the "crack in the door," so to speak, that many of the scammers walked in through.

In addition to that, people who forward these e-mails look a bit foolish, so it is always a good idea to spend at least a little time fact checking before you click the Send button.

One of the best places to verify whether that e-mail you just received is true is http://www.snopes.com. This site has an encyclopedic listing of urban legends with descriptions of the stories and verification of whether the story is true (or whether the story is unverified). One of the best things they do at this site is debunk fake news stories that have a real but unrelated photo associated with them (typically someone makes up a story around a photo and it gets forwarded as news). The folks who contribute to the Snopes site are also good at identifying photos that have been altered with a photo editor.

E-Mail Stock Tips (Pump-and-Dump Scams)

One of the major changes made possible by the Internet is the number of people who invest in and trade stocks. It seems that just about everybody we know has some investments in stocks, whereas 20 years ago it was something that only wealthy people did. The reason for the boom in investing is twofold. First, the Internet made it easy for people to invest. No calls or visits to a brokerage, just point and click. Second, at the same time that most people received such online access to investing, the stock market hit an unprecedented period of growth (the so-called "bubble" in the late 1990s).

So far, this is all good. The problem with the situation though is that a lot of people out there have no idea what they are doing when it comes to investing. This creates a great opportunity for scammers to take advantage of people who invest without researching the stocks they are purchasing.

The scam involves what is known as a "pump and dump." The bad guys start by throwing a little money into a stock. Then they "pump up" a relatively worthless stock by hyping it up on chat boards or in this case by sending out millions of e-mails. This creates a buzz about the stock, and more folks who do not want to miss out on such an "opportunity" start buying. It looks like the stock is getting hot, which drives the price up. This attracts new investors whose investments also temporarily drive the stock price up again, and so on. At this point, the scammers sell all their shares for a nice profit. Usually within days, the price comes crashing down because there was little or no value in the company's stock to begin with.

This scam is surprisingly effective using e-mail. One of the tactics used quite a bit is the "accidental" e-mail, where it is made to seem like a hot stock tip was meant for someone else. Usually there is a hint of insider information that the stock is about to take off.

Please heed this advice: If you invest in stocks based solely on an anonymous tip, whether it comes via e-mail or is overheard in a bathroom stall or on a train, you are not an investor, you are a gambler. And not a very good one either.

If you do want to invest and are looking for information on a prospective stock, either consult reputable professionals at the brokerage of your choice or go to a site such as the following:

    http://www.sec.gov/edgar.shtml

And, get good, solid information. If you want to gamble, go to Vegas.

Work from Home (Pyramid) Schemes

Job boards and e-mail solicitations are full of offers to work from home and make thousands per week. These used to come in the mail and in the back of every supermarket gossip rag. With e-mail and the Internet, the cost of running such schemes came down to fractions of pennies.

These "opportunities" are usually pyramid schemes in which people who have previously been duped get paid to dupe other people. After the first few rounds, the whole thing collapses. Sometimes, the initiators of the scams get busted for fraud; with the Internet, however, it is much easier to start a sham business in countries with weak extradition laws.

Our advice: If you want to work at home, fantastic. But, consult a legitimate job site such as the following:

    http://www.monster.com

Money-Exchange Schemes

A money-exchange scheme is a scam in which the victim is notified that a large amount of cash is being held for them, usually in a foreign bank. Victims are told that to get the cash out, a retainer must be set up, which when paid will free up the cash for them. By putting up the cash upfront, victims are told they will receive a cut of the cash being transferred. In some cases, the perpetrators ask for the victim's bank account and routing number so that they can "easily deposit the money."

There are variations on this theme with regard to the story wrapped around the scam. Sometimes, a rich relative has died, and you have been identified as the sole heir. Sometimes, a small organization is notified, perhaps a church, that some rich foreigner wanted to leave the cash to it. No matter the story, it is all a scam. These people will take the upfront retainer money the victim gives them and disappear.

For some reason, Nigeria is often the country used in the scam, so much so that the scam is also called a Nigerian bank scam. It can and does originate in a lot of places, however, so do not fall for it. If you are approached via e-mail or by phone about one of these "opportunities," contact the authorities. The SEC and the FBI are good places to start.

"Hot" Merchandise Scam

Another scam making its way around is the "hot" merchandise scam. In this one, victims are asked to agree to have some merchandise sent to their residence. The reason given is usually that the person ordering the stuff is in transit or because he is ordering a gift for someone who lives with him and he wants to keep it a secret. The victim is usually offered some money in exchange for the service.

The scam is that the merchandise is often purchased with bad checks or stolen credit cards. The thieves will come to your house, collect their stuff from you, and then disappear.

Although you may in fact get paid for your service, the paper trail of the ill-gotten gains leads the authorities to your door, leaving you to explain what happened. Oh, and by the way, if you notify the authorities after you have been hit, these people now know where you live. Also, good luck cashing that check they gave you. It is probably about as good as the credit cards they used.

What to Do to Protect Yourself

The most important thing you can do to protect yourself online is to use common sense and have a good amount of healthy skepticism. Keep in mind that although you might not ever fall for one of these scams, members for your family or friends might, so it is worth talking about. Here are some guidelines to follow:

- Verify your facts before you pass along information or deal with an individual or business online. You can find a lot of information by searching on Google.com. The time you spend there could save you a lot of time, money, and embarrassment.

- Remember when you "meet" somebody online that you do not "know" that person. It is a simple matter to disguise yourself online. The person you are dealing with could be anybody from anywhere.

- Do not give anyone your personal information unless you are 100 percent certain they are legitimate.

- Ask yourself the following question: If you were outside your home and a stranger offered you the same deal in a mall or on a street that you are being offered via e-mail or online, would you take it? Then why would you take it online?

- Remember that if something sounds too good to be true, it is.

- Listen to your gut. If something feels wrong about a person or situation you are dealing with, walk away from it.

- Invoke the "24-hour rule." Close that laptop or shut down that computer and sleep on it.

- Do not let greed or ego get the best of you. They are the very weaknesses scammers rely on to nail you. There is no such thing as a risk-free investment.

- Before you commit to anything, talk about it with someone you know and trust. Use your friends or family as a sounding board.

- If you think you have received a scam e-mail, report it to the authorities. In the United States, you can report scams at http://www.ic3.gov.

Summary

Unlike the other chapters in this book, there is nothing to hook up or enable on your computer or home network when it comes to common sense (although we wish we could bottle some and sell it).

A lot of people, even smart people, get burned by online scams every year. Both of us have received plenty of e-mails from college graduates with warnings to be careful on business trips lest we wake up missing a kidney and in a bathtub, information about a secret Neiman Marcus cookie recipe, notification that Bill Gates is giving away money, and, oh my, an avalanche of stock tips.

Just remember that it takes a willing victim for a scam to work. A little time, effort, and a healthy dose of common sense can keep you out of trouble.

Where to Go for More Information

The *Securities and Exchange Commission* (SEC) offers some good information about online scams and Internet fraud:

> http://www.sec.gov/investor/pubs/cyberfraud.htm

The U.S. Department of Justice also provides some good information on their site:

> http://www.internetfraud.usdoj.gov/

For a nongovernment perspective, you can visit Scam Busters, which also provides some excellent information:

> http://www.scambusters.org

CHAPTER 11

"They Couldn't Hit an Elephant at This Distance"

"They couldn't hit an elephant at this distance." The last words of Major-General John Sedgewick, shot dead in front of his troops while defiantly strutting around in plain sight of the enemy line, berating their shooting abilities.

Complacency in home security is dangerous. A little hard work (and humility) can go a long way toward making yourself less of a target. Securing your home network does not have to be complicated. We have given you 10 solid tips for what to do, and most of them are pretty straightforward.

As a final note, it is important to understand that security threats and security tips are not a one-to-one mapping. In other words, each security tip helps protect against multiple types of threats. As well, each threat sometimes takes more than one security tip to protect yourself against it.

It is a bit like your home security. Locking the front door protects you against home invaders, trespassers, and people stealing your wallet and your DVD player. However, you also need to lock the windows, the garage, and maybe install an alarm system.

Home network security is the same. Threats can enter your computers in multiple ways. All 10 security tips that we have presented here work together in concert to protect against many types of threats, and you should follow all 10.

Table 11-1 shows how the different security tips relate to several common threats. The table shows both which threats a security tip helps protect against and which security tips are needed to protect against a specific threat.

Table 11-1   Threats and Tips

Threats \ Security Tips	Use Firewalls	Secure Your Wireless Network	Use Antivirus Protection	Keep Your Software Updated	Lock Out Spyware and Adware	Keep an Eye on Your Kids	Recognize and Avoid Phishing Scams	Create Strong Passwords	Back Up Your Files	Use Common Sense
Viruses Causing Problems on Your Computers	▓		▓	▓	▓				▓	▓
Illegal Activity Using Your Network for Anonymity	▓	▓	▓	▓	▓		▓	▓		▓
Critical Data and File Loss	▓	▓	▓	▓	▓		▓	▓	▓	▓
Slow Computer Performance	▓		▓	▓	▓			▓		▓
Invasion of Privacy	▓	▓	▓	▓	▓		▓	▓	▓	▓
Identity Theft and Financial Loss	▓	▓	▓	▓			▓	▓	▓	▓
Children Exposed to Adult Content	▓	▓	▓	▓	▓	▓	▓	▓	▓	▓

As one example, let's consider computer viruses. The obvious security tip to protect against this threat is to install and use antivirus software on your computers. However, as discussed in Chapter 3, "Tip 3: Use Antivirus Protection," antivirus software is not 100-percent effective. We also need firewalls to prevent intrusions and to block malicious programs from accessing the Internet. Keeping the operating system updated also reduces the holes in the software that a virus can exploit. Common sense can help prevent you from opening that e-mail containing the virus in the first place. And, if all else fails, having a backup of your computer can save your butt when all lines of defense have failed and the virus wrecks your computer.

So, please follow all 10 tips. If you do, you will not be bullet-proof, but at least you will be as secure as someone can be without spending a ton of money (and much more secure than the average Internet user).

We leave you with a final thought. There's a joke that goes something like this:

> Two guys are out walking in the woods and they come across a pretty angry bear. One guy freezes; the other starts lacing up his running shoes. His friend stops panicking for a minute and asks, "Why are you doing that? Do you really think you can outrun a bear?" The other guy says, "I don't need to outrun the bear. I just need to outrun you."

Home network security is no different. Lace up your shoes.

Numerals

2.4 GHz

Operating frequency shared by cordless telephones, wireless home networks (WLAN or WiFi), and unfortunately microwave ovens and other devices that can cause interference.

5.8 GHz

Operating frequency for newer cordless telephones and wireless home networks (WLAN or WiFi), with less interference (yet) from other devices.

A

ad hoc

Refers to a wireless network that is computer to computer, without a wireless router.

adware

Programs that are designed to display advertising to the user that may not be expected or wanted.

annoyware

This special type of adware causes an excessive number of popups/popunders and is designed to force advertising even when not connected to the Internet. It can cause noticeable system and bandwidth slowdowns and in general is intrusive to the point of frustrating the system user.

antispyware/antiadware

Software programs used to detect, remove, and prevent adware and spyware programs from being installed on computer systems.

antivirus

Software programs used to detect, remove, and prevent computer viruses, worms, and Trojan horses from being installed on computer systems.

B

backup

The process of copying critical files to another device or location to protect against the loss of data in the event of a file-destroying virus, loss, or physical trauma to a computer.

banner ads

Can be either a legitimate advertisement on a web page or a misleading ad designed to get the user to click it thinking it is part of the web page or a Windows dialog box.

bit

Short for "binary unit" (or binary digit); this is single digit of information, which is a 1 or 0.

blog

Short for web log, a website on which items are posted on a regular basis and displayed in reverse chronological order.

bot

Programs that install themselves on people's computers for malicious purposes, often used as remote-attack tools to allow a hacker to gain control over your computer.

bot army

Thousands of computers that have been taken over by hackers remotely, typically to anonymously conduct distributed denial-of-service attacks.

broadband

A term used to describe high-speed Internet service. The term comes from the fact that a broad range of frequencies are used to attain high information-exchange rates.

browser

A program used to access content on the Internet. Examples include Internet Explorer, Firefox, Netscape, and Opera.

brute-force attack

Defeating password or encrypted data by successively trying a large number of possibilities (for example, exhaustively trying password combinations using a dictionary attack program).

byte

A standard-size "chunk" of computer language or network information. A byte is made of 8 bits.

C

cable

Can refer to a wire with connectors to connect two devices together or can refer to the type of broadband service you get from your cable TV provider.

chat

Instant messaging session in which often three or more people are involved.

D

denial-of-service (DoS) attack

An attack on a computer system or network that causes a loss of service to users by consuming the bandwidth of the network or overloading the processor and memory of the computer system.

DHCP (Dynamic Host Configuration Protocol)

This protocol is used by service providers and network equipment to automatically assign random IP addresses from a pool rather than assigning permanent IP addresses to users.

dictionary attack

Password-cracking attempts that successively tries possibilities that are most likely to succeed, typically derived from a list of words in a dictionary. Generally, dictionary attacks succeed because most people have a tendency to choose passwords that are easy to remember.

distributed denial-of-service (DDoS) attack

Using hundreds or thousands of computers that have been taken over (*see* bot army) to conduct a DoS attack on a corporation, government entity, or website service with the intent to cause severe service disruption or complete failure.

downlink

The connection and information flow from the service provider to your computer.

drive-by download

The act of prompting the user to download a program while browsing the Internet without the user ever requesting installation of the program in the first place.

DSL (digital subscriber line)

A high-speed Internet connection that uses unused frequencies on phone lines to deliver very high data rates with the use of a specialized modem.

DVD (digital video disc)

An optical storage disc and media format that can be used for data storage, including for movies with high video and sound quality.

dynamic IP address

Having an IP address assigned by a device in the Internet service provider's network, which can change each time an address is requested. Often referred to as DHCP, which is the name of the protocol that specifies the rules for allocating IP addresses in this manner.

E

e-mail

An application used to exchange notes and files between two or more people. An e-mail is identified by the username and the service provider, such as bob@network.com. Applications include Microsoft Outlook, Eudora, Hotmail, and others.

Ethernet

A protocol that defines the rules for computer communication over certain types of networks. It is the dominant protocol in use for both home and businesses.

eyeballs

Measure of how many people's eyes view a particular advertisement on a web page or popup ad. We think they only count pairs.

F

firewall
A physical device or software program that prevents unwanted access into a private network from an outside location.

Flash memory
A rewriteable memory chip that functions very similarly to a disk drive, used by computers, cameras, MP3 players, and mobile phones to store digital media. These are often referred to memory keys, memory sticks, or USB keys.

FTP (File Transfer Protocol)
This protocol is used to copy files between computers over the Internet.

G

Gb (Gigabit)
1 billion bits.

GB (Gigabyte)
1,073,741,824 bytes.

GHz (gigahertz)
Measurement of a radio frequency equating to one billion cycles per second.

Google
A website used to search for topics or other sites. Its popularity has made it a verb meaning "to search," such as "I googled Geek Squad."

H

hack
A clever or elegant modification to computer software to gain unauthorized access or otherwise cause computer software to malfunction.

hacker
A person able to exploit a computer system or gain unauthorized access, usually by creating or modifying computer software.

heuristics
Process where information about known viruses is used to attempt detection of unknown or suspected viruses, attempting to halt viruses based on their behavior instead of exact signature.

hijacker
Applications that are designed to hijack the user's home page, HOSTS file, browser favorites, chosen search engine, or system settings.

hotspot
A wireless network available for use in a public place such as a coffee shop or airport.

HTTP (Hypertext Transfer Protocol)
This is the computer communication language used to retrieve information from web pages written in certain "markup" languages.

I

IM (instant messaging)
IM is quickly becoming one of the most popular forms of communication over the Internet and cell phone networks. Examples include MSN Messenger, GoogleTalk, and Yahoo! Messenger.

Internet
This is the worldwide system of computer networks. Although many private networks connect to it, the Internet is public, cooperative, and self-sustaining.

IP (Internet Protocol)
Defines the communication rules for devices on the Internet. Communication within this protocol is based on the assignment of IP addresses.

IP address
Numeric address by which computers, web servers, and devices are known by on the Internet. IP addresses have little bearing on geographic location, although some blocks of addresses can be linked to regions or states.

ISP (Internet service provider)
A company that provides access to the Internet for residential or business use.

K–L

keylogger
Applications that are designed to record and/or transmit keystroke information.

kilobit (Kb)
1000 bits. This is a standard transmission rate unit for dialup modems when referred to over a portion of time such as Kbps or kilobits per second.

kilobyte (KB)
1024 bytes.

LAN (local-area network)
This is small network within a house, department, or business.

M–N

MAC (Media Access Control) address
The unique physical serial number given by the manufacturer to every networking device used for network communication.

megabit (Mb)
1 million bits. When measured over time, this is the standard transmission rate unit for high-speed modems.

megabyte (MB)
1,048,576 bytes.

modem (modulator demodulator)
Devices that translate computer language for transmission over a communication line (such as a phone line) and back again.

Network Address Translation (NAT)
A home router translates the private IP addresses used by computers on your home network to a single public IP address assigned to your broadband modem, providing the ability for multiple computers to share a connection and also providing a degree of privacy because the computers on your home network are not able to be accessed directly from the Internet.

NIC (network interface card)
Provides the connection for a computer to either a wired or wireless network. Can be installed internally to the computer (PCI), connected externally to a USB port, or plugged into the PCMCIA slot of a laptop.

P

parental control
Software program or service that allows parents to control child access to the Internet.

peer to peer
Another term for ad-hoc wireless networking, whereby two computers establish a connection directly to each other without a wireless access point.

phishing
Sending e-mail pretending to be a legitimate business to perpetrate a scam on the receiver, such as stealing identities, credit card information, or login account and password.

ping
Utility program on most PCs that can be used to test a network connection.

popup blocker
Program or Internet browser feature that prevents popup ads from being displayed on a computer user's screen.

R

redirect

Intentionally changing the destination of a website to a different address than originally entered by the user.

registry

A database that stores settings and options for the Microsoft Windows operating system, containing information and settings for all the hardware, software, users, and preferences of the PC.

restore point

Checkpoint in the Windows operating system that allows restoring to a previous point in time, like an "undo" function.

router

A networking device that makes "intelligent" decisions regarding how traffic is moved across or through a network.

S

scanning

Searching the memory and disk drives of a computer (usually by an antivirus program) for malicious software, such as viruses, worms, and Trojan horses.

signature

The computer code fingerprint for a virus, worm, Trojan horse, adware, or spyware program that allows it to be identified by an antivirus or antispyware/antiadware program.

Skype

Popular, free Internet-based voice chat service.

spam

Unsolicited e-mail sent to thousands of people in attempts to advertise a product, promote a stock, or launch a scam.

spyware

Software that is designed to collect information in secret, might or might not install in stealth, and is designed to transmit that information to second or third parties covertly employing users' Internet connections without their consent and knowledge.

SSID (service set identifier)

A term used for the name of a WLAN.

stateful packet inspection (SPI)

Examining each packet that flows through a firewall to make sure the packet is a) in response to a legitimate request by a computer on the home network and b) the correct packet in the expected sequence of packets.

static IP address

Having an IP address assigned by the Internet service provider, which does not change.

T

TCP (Transmission Control Protocol)

A subset Internet Protocol (IP) set of rules to send data in the form of message units between computers over the Internet.

TiVo

Service that allows digital recording of live TV, also known as DVR (digital video recorder). Warning: The authors have found TiVo to be highly addictive.

Trojan horse

Type of computer virus that deposits a back door on a computer system so that a hacker can take control of the computer remotely over the Internet.

U

uplink

Refers to the data flow from the computer to the service provider (and then to the Internet).

urban legend

A kind of folklore consisting of stories often thought to be factual by those circulating them. Urban legends are not necessarily untrue, but they are often false, distorted, exaggerated, or sensationalized.

URL (universal record locator)

The official term for a link to a website or other material on the Internet, also known as the web address.

USB (universal serial bus)

An interface that allows other devices to be connected and disconnected without resetting the system. Also a serial communication standard that allows high-speed data communication to many devices.

V

virus

A self-replicating/self-reproducing-automation program that spreads by inserting copies of itself into other executable code or documents.

VoIP (Voice over IP)

A collection of protocols for transporting voice conversations across a data network. Also known as IP Telephony.

VoIP chat

Using the Internet for voice conversations and phone calls, for which there is typically no number to call, but you reach others through their "handle," much like instant messaging. Online gaming systems, such as Xbox Live, often provide a voice chat feature for players to communicate during games.

W

web server

A very fast computer that handles requests for web pages.

WEP (Wired Equivalency Protocol)

Encryption security standard for 802.11-based wireless home networks.

worm

A computer worm is a self-replicating computer program, similar to a computer virus. A worm is self-contained and does not need to be part of another program to propagate itself.

WPA (Wi-Fi Protected Access)

More-recent encryption security standard for 802.11-based wireless home networks, considered more secure than WEP.

WPA2 (Wi-Fi Protected Access 2)

Latest encryption security standard for 802.11-based wireless home networks, considered more secure than WEP and WPA. Provides for periodic key rotation during a session.

INDEX

005.8   Doherty, Jim, CCNA.
DOH
           Home network security
             simplified.

$19.99

DATE			

WITHDRAWN

LONGWOOD PUBLIC LIBRARY
MIDDLE COUNTRY RD
MIDDLE ISLAND NY 11953

08/03/2006

BAKER & TAYLOR